LIVE GRATEFULLY

A JOURNEY WITHIN

·

·

·

MIRJANA BOZNOVSKA

Copyright © Mirjana Boznovska, 2020

All rights reserved. No part of this publication may be reproduced, distributed, or transmitted in any form or by any means, including photocopying, recording, or other electronic or mechanical methods, without the prior written permission of the publisher, except in the case of brief quotations embodied in critical reviews and certain other non-commercial uses permitted by copyright law. For permission requests, write to the publisher at: mirjana@mirjana.co

Published by Conscious Life Media consciouslifemedia.com

Purchase your copy at: www.mirjana.co

The author of this book does not dispense medical advice, nor prescribe the use of any technique as a form of treatment for physical or medical problems without the consent of a physician, either indirectly or directly. The intent of the author is only to offer information of a general nature to help you in the quest for vitality and wellbeing. In the event you use any of the information in this book for yourself, the author and the publisher assume no responsibility for your actions. By reading further, you agree to this in its entirety.

Edition 1, 2020

ISBN 978-0-6489374-0-1 (sc)

ISBN 978-0-6489374-1-8 (e)

*The path isn't a straight line, it's a spiral.
You continually come back
to things you thought you understood
and see deeper and deeper truths.*

CONTENTS

∙

∙

∙

INTRODUCTION	10
WHO AM I?	14
WHAT IS GRATITUDE REALLY?	18

CHAPTER 1: MY JOURNEY — 22

The Innocence of Early Childhood	23
Never Seen, Never Heard	25
From Young Adult to New Mum	27
The Pain of a Miscarriage	28
Everything In Between Up to Now	31
Beauty Behind Every Tear You Cry	34

CHAPTER 2: SELF WORTH — 36

God's Unconditional Love	39
Romantic Love	39
Friendships	41
Happiness	43
Truth Is Your Compass Home	43
One of a Kind — Yes, That's You!	45
Have You Lost Yourself in Motherhood, Marriage and Career?	47
Your Value Is Intrinsic: You Were Born with It	49
Beauty Starts on the Inside	49
A Confident Woman: Perception Versus Reality	51
You Are the Fairytale Story	53
True Friends	55
What Is Self-Love?	55
Relationships: Your Posture of Love	55
True Friendships	59

CHAPTER 3: STRENGTH — 60

Emotional Pain: Acceptance	61
Emotional Pain: Resilience	61
The Power of Choice: Own It!	63
Tree of Life and Love	65

Lioness Arising ... 67
Don't Underestimate Your Courage ... 67
In the Midst of Darkness Your Light Will Prevail ... 71
Never Ever, Ever Give Up ... 71
Whatever Your Season, You're Not Alone ... 73
The Person Behind the Mask ... 75
What Did You Do for Someone Else Today? ... 77
Sorry! Just Another Word in Our Vocabulary? ... 79
Kneel in the Dark So You Can Stand in the Dark ... 81
Are You on the Regret Highway? ... 81
It's Your Time to Fly ... 83
Be Still: Find Your *Being-ness* ... 85
Empowerment: The New Age Buzzword ... 87
The Healing Power of Forgiving ... 89

CHAPTER 4: PURPOSE ... 92

What Do You Want to Be Remembered For? ... 93
Your Dream Is Your Destiny ... 93
Happiness: It's All That Matters ... 97
The River Flows in You ... 97
Are You Waiting for Something? ... 99
What on Earth Am I Here For? ... 99
Open Your Heart to Love ... 101
Boldness Is Your Calling ... 103
Knowledge Is Enlightenment ... 105
Dreams Are Cultivated in the Right Environment ... 105
Ego: An Illusion or Real? ... 107
Being Called: Step Out in Faith ... 109
To Love and to Be Loved ... 111
Ethics and Values: Can They Be Compromised? ... 111
Think Helping—Less Selling ... 113
To Be Truly Fulfilled, We Need Others ... 115

CHAPTER 5: A PERSONAL EXPERIENCE ... 118

A Child's Perspective: Uninhibited, Raw and True ... 121
A Child's Insight: How Blessed ... 123
Enduring Love ... 125

CHAPTER 6: HEALTH AND WELLNESS — 128

Your Journey to Health and Wellness Starts Now — 129
Listen to Your Body: Sometimes You Just Have to *Be* — 131
Have You Forgotten *Why* You Should Be Happy? — 133
Why Have We Overcomplicated Healthy Living? — 135
Walk and Talk Club: Start Now — 137
Seeking a Makeover to Make You Feel Better? — 139
Health and Wellness Is More Than a Weight Loss Journey — 139
Why You Should Not Skip Breakfast — 141
Naked Perspective: How Do You Really See Yourself? — 143
Imagine the Possibilities — 145

CHAPTER 7: HOW TO MAKE A CHANGE — 146

Opening the Door to Change — 147
Step out of Chaos and into Harmony — 147
Get out of the Toxic Relationship with Yourself — 149
To Be Remembered — 153
Get Back on Track — 155
Life Is a Blank Canvas: What Will You Paint? — 157
To Live Gratefully: A Male Perspective — 157
Turn Down the Noise in Your Life—To Reveal Your Truth — 159
Your Thoughts Predetermine the Quality of Your Life — 163
Transformation Starts in the Mind — 163
Unclutter Your Mind: Unclutter Your Life — 165
Your Smile Is More Precious Than Any Diamond — 165
Discover Who Are You — 167
Listen to Your Soul — 169
Accept Your Life Unconditionally — 171
Practical Steps to Make a Change — 171
Never, Ever, Ever Give Up — 173

THANK YOU — 174

ABOUT THE AUTHOR — 176

Mirjana's specialties — 180
Inquiries — 182

INTRODUCTION

INTRODUCTION

This book has been an incredible way for me to document the journey from lowest of lows to a life of deep calm and gratitude. While it is a collection of Facebook posts, a selection of my personal diary entries and further writings, it is much more than that. I believe this book has reached you for a reason: perhaps you're needing assurance of better things to come, when things don't seem to be going how you'd like. Sometimes we just need a friend—a shoulder to lean on—inspiration to pick us up and help us find the silver lining. It is my sincere hope within these pages you find exactly what you need, when you need it.

I have an affinity with lost and hurting women. This book is dedicated to you, but also to all of the hurting men in our society. I want to say to you, whatever your story, your experience, whatever your pain, whatever your shame, whatever your betrayal, whatever your guilt... the numbness you may feel right now that may have resulted in the loss of your identity and self-worth—I understand it, I get you! There is absolutely a way to move past this pain. *Know and believe* you will move past it and flourish in your own amazing way.

INTRODUCTION

"

*Eventually
people will notice your light,
ask about you,
want to get to know you,
your choices,
your story...
you will be of interest to them
and will be in a position
to make a positive influence.*

*The deepest courage of all
is to show up,
be seen and declare
"This is Who I Am".
This is the truest essence
of beautiful.*

*Live fearlessly,
Live playfully,
Live peacefully.*

INTRODUCTION

My hope is by being transparent about my story you will find healing for your past, restoration for your present and inspiration for your future.

Believe. Sometimes we go through life within the safe parameters of our comfort zone. This may be by personal choice, by ignorance, or because of life circumstances beyond our control. We end up living a life less fulfilling than we intended. Whatever the scenario, your story, your experience, your journey is valuable and it has the capacity to make a difference in the world. Our negatives can become powerful tools that can bring inspiration, hope and healing to others. The testimony of the Lord is the wonderful story of God at work in your life. *Believe*.

WHO AM I?

.

.

.

WHO AM I?

My journey has been a rollercoaster of highs and lows. However, I would not change that for the world. I know and truly believe my journey has shaped me into who I am today. I also know and believe *my past does not define me.* Rather it has allowed me to experience spiritual growth and maturity. My journey has allowed me to peel back opinions, including social, cultural and associated conditioning imposed by each of them. In the process, I have become more accepting of who I am and comfortable standing in my own truth.

The road I have travelled has taken me from working as an accountant to the health and wellness field, with an emphasis on emotional health and wellbeing. I am excited, encouraged and truly humbled at the opportunity to present to you my story.

My intention for this book is to share and express thoughts that have helped me navigate my own journey in life. I have compiled all these posts in this book as a keepsake to treasure. My hope is that you are able to connect to the message in my writings and that in the process you encounter the Holy Spirit and God's grace in your life.

> *The relationship we have*
> *to our own heart and mind*
> *sets the tone for how we will*
> *experience the world around us.*
>
> *The human condition is the same,*
> *irrespective of gender, status,*
> *occupation or financial position.*
> *The human condition asks:*
>
> *Who am I?*
> *Why am I here?*
> *What is my purpose?*
>
> *The problems of humanity*
> *cannot be fixed*
> *unless we awaken*
> *the beautiful hearts of humanity.*

I wish to express a heartfelt thank you in advance for connecting to the messages in my posts and sharing them with your family and friends. I feel blessed to be in a position of being able to inspire and provide hope and direction to you during what might be a difficult season in your life.

My inspiration for my posts is to glorify the name of God and His wonderful work in my life. God has wonderful plans for your life, too. Be blessed.

WHAT IS GRATITUDE REALLY?

.
.
.

To live gratefully, in an authentic way, is to appreciate you have been blessed with a beautiful life. This gives purpose and meaning to everything you do. It shifts your focus from what you don't have to the many blessings that are already around you.

Being grateful makes you happier and more resilient to setbacks. It also reduces stress and improves your relationships with yourself and others. All this affects you positively. The net result: improved overall health, vitality and wellbeing.

A grateful heart is one filled with joy, love and happiness for where you are right now in your life.

To live gratefully means:

- Value and appreciate your blessings. Rather than think of what you don't have, appreciate what you have.

- Keep things simple. Gratitude flourishes in the simplicity of life.

- Accept that blessings are not always found in material things. Endearing qualities of grace, empathy, compassion and humility allow you to express love towards yourself and others.

> *Gratitude is a fullness of heart*
> *that transcends all things.*
> *It moves you from limitation,*
> *fear and regret to love,*
> *joy and limitlessness.*
>
> *If you allow yourself to feel all feelings*
> *without judgement,*
> *you become deeply grateful*
> *and appreciate more fully what you have*
> *rather than focusing on what you want*
> *all of the time.*
> *This type of gratitude allows*
> *for all the other fears and feelings*
> *of anxiety to fall away—an awakening*
> *of reorientating priorities.*
> *It seems to wipe out all that isn't important*
> *and leaves you with clarity*
> *for what is most important in your life right now.*

- Speak the words *thank you* often. These words have power and magic. When they are said with sincerity, they become magnetic and memorable. They almost become a physical thing. A thank you energises and radiates warmth. When you speak these words, you attract warmth and energy in return.

- Reach out to those less fortunate and in need; never underestimate the difference you can make in the lives of others through a simple chat or a hug or a cup of tea or a few moments of your time. You can magnify their strengths by genuinely listening to their story or by giving a compliment or a smile. Everyone can use a helping hand now and then.

- Smile more often as smiling shows gratitude and grows connection: Your smile is more precious than any diamond. It has the power to influence perspective and provide hope and it can change the world, including your own.

Cultivate gratitude to appreciate that your life is beautiful *now*. No matter how hard your day, week, month, year, or journey has been, find something to be grateful for. Inspire someone by living gratefully, despite what is happening in outside circumstances.

CHAPTER 1

. . .

MY JOURNEY

CHAPTER 1: MY JOURNEY

One evening in the midst of deep despair, I experienced a wonderful revelation that my story and journey have been for a purpose: to bring hope to others, to be a beacon of light that shines so brightly that it inspires others to want to make a change. I do not have all the answers, nor do I want to pretend to be an expert in life matters. In fact, I am still on my own journey of self-discovery. Sharing my story shows my vulnerability and imperfections, my wounds and scars, and I'm totally comfortable and accepting of that. My hope is in doing so it gives you strength for what you have faced in your past and for what you are facing right now and that it is possible to move past this point so you do not continue to face it in the future.

The symbolism of my journey is one of transformation from caterpillar to butterfly and in the process finding and developing an intimate connection with God or as some like to refer, their higher power or universal truth. This has resulted in a renewed lease on life, passion and determination that have enabled me to have hope and believe in the life I was always meant to live.

My mission is to empower women and men to want to make a change, to be at their personal best physically, emotionally and spiritually so that they also can experience a renewed lease on life, passion and determination—so that they too can lead the life they were always meant to live and be a source of inspiration to others.

We all have a stewardship of responsibility to help and inspire others and my hope is that by sharing my story you will see hope, determination, faith, salvation, grace, love, compassion and forgiveness.

THE INNOCENCE OF EARLY CHILDHOOD

We threw sheets over the chairs and lay our little heads on the sofa cushions placed underneath. We had beanies and gloves on and huddled under a warm blanket. It was a freezing cold day. We giggled and told stories as we pretended to be camping. In fact,

CHAPTER 1: MY JOURNEY

"

*The relationship we have to ourselves
is what gives us the foundation
to stand in our wholeness
with or without a partner,
to trust that we are and have always been
enough, worthy and lovable as we are.*

we were camping in our living room. My sister and I played well growing up. She was the boss and I did as I was told. And that's how it worked. I was the youngest of my parent's two daughters.

We played imaginative games with what was around the house. We didn't have many toys and made the most of what we had. We made dolls with blankets and tea towels and aprons wrapped around them. We played school. She was the teacher and I always had to be the student—I guess because she was older.

My memories of early school days are quite blurred, neither happy nor unhappy. Mum and Dad worked hard, so often my sister and I walked to and from school from a young age and remained at home until my parents arrived from work. We were given a huge responsibility of self-care from early childhood.

NEVER SEEN, NEVER HEARD

High school was a different environment. I was invisible—not to be seen, not to be heard. I excelled academically but was socially isolated and insecure. There was so much pressure growing up—and there still is—in terms of what we should look like, what we should wear, what we should seem to be doing. It was and remains commercialised and predetermined by the media, society and our own culture.

I was the chubby, unpopular kid, and not many knew my name. I often tried to look busy by going to the library during school lunch time. This was a silent time in my life. I was unable to express myself and was often teased about my weight and body shape. The interesting thing was even then I would say to myself, *"It's okay, hang in there. One day things will be different."*

Teenage years can be difficult and I want to say to you who are reading this book, if you are a teenager or young adult experiencing this pain, stay firm in your belief you are awesome, beautiful and wonderful as you are. Do not give your power away to others by letting them determine how you should think about yourself.

CHAPTER 1: MY JOURNEY

❝

*When you leave
family programming unchecked,
you can end up repeating the experiences
of those who came before you.*

So, you have some weight to lose, weight to gain, you are short, you are tall, your hair is light or dark, or your eyes are brown or blue. Are you getting what I am saying? People will always find something to focus on, compare or complain about.

Do not let others dim your light. You are fearfully and wonderfully made and you are beautiful just as you are. Know that and believe in that always.

FROM YOUNG ADULT TO NEW MUM

I remember seeing my dad beam proudly as I accepted my certificate. They called my name as I graduated with a Bachelor of Business credit. My dad was a gentle, soft-natured person. I say *was* because he has passed away. He left the most amazing legacy: never, ever give up. Despite what you are faced with, you go on and continue to do your best.

My parents were strict as we were growing up, and I found I didn't have a very close relationship at the time as they just didn't get me. I felt they didn't really understand my pain of social isolation. I wasn't allowed much of a social life or interaction. I would graduate from childhood to become married and raising a young family, in my early twenties.

My four children—Danny, Caroline, Tiana and Emily—are my most amazing achievements and contribution to this world that I have made and will ever make. Every day they give me hope and inspiration to be the best mum that I can be, and their unconditional love and support is a blessing. What I am most grateful for is their compassion, humility and consideration for others. These values I hold dear to my heart, and I am truly grateful to God for the honour and privilege of raising these four amazing children.

They are extremely close siblings despite the significant age differences between the first two and the younger children. I hold the concept of family dear to my heart. Hopefully I have influenced their values in this area. Over and above the achievement of academic accolades, the values that I hold most dear to my heart and have encouraged my children to adopt are generosity, ethics, kindness and compassion towards others.

THE PAIN OF A MISCARRIAGE

Time stood still that horrible day, as the doctor's words echoed in my head: "I can't find the heartbeat", he said.

I stared in shock at the ultrasound machine. My mind screamed, *what are you saying?* There was no voice coming from my mouth. I stared at the screen, willing the heartbeat to start up again. Just a month earlier, I had seen my little baby move and blood flowing to his precious heart. *Please, please,* my heart cried, *please find it.*

"Try again. Perhaps you have missed it," I begged him. The world had seemed to stop suddenly and there was nothing more to hear or see. My beautiful little boy was gone at twenty-three weeks.

It hurt so badly that I didn't know what to do. I blamed myself. *Why, why, why didn't I know sooner what had happened? Maybe I could have stopped it from happening. Was it my fault?* These questions kept screaming over and over in my head.

I felt that nobody understood my pain. This was not a lost pregnancy or stillborn as some had described it. This was my precious little boy.

CHAPTER 1: MY JOURNEY

To my beautiful little boy Jamie:

*I'm sorry I didn't get to hold you
and whisper I love you.
I was never ready for you to leave me.
Some would say I didn't even know you, but I did.
I did know you and I fell in love with you.
Your life, though brief, will not be without meaning.
You will change the world
because your existence changed me.
I rejoice in your life
and that all you will ever know is
love, joy and peace
nestled in the arms of your creator, our God.
One day we will meet again, my beautiful boy.
You are always in my heart,
Mummy Mirjana.*

> *The first step is becoming aware
> of the underlying pre-made choices
> you've been set up with throughout your life.
> The greatest step towards success and long-term change
> is the recognition of your own dysfunction
> assumed as a result of generational conditioning
> and the blueprint of the ego.*

CHAPTER 1: MY JOURNEY

EVERYTHING IN BETWEEN UP TO NOW

For the last five years I have been on a journey of self-discovery with an emphasis on physical, emotional, and spiritual health and wellbeing. All my life I have struggled to lose weight. I had constantly been on diets. I've had no energy and low self-esteem and have been highly stressed while trying to manage the balance of work and life as a mother of four children and juggling a career in business.

Five years ago, I stopped to ask myself: *Mirjana, are you at your personal best physically, emotionally and spiritually?*

This question was confrontational. My answer was even more confrontational. Not only was I *not* at my personal best, but I was emotionally numb, lived on autopilot and was living an unhealthy, toxic lifestyle fuelled by poor diet, an inactive, as well as negative and unhealthy mindset.

Physically, I was 40 kilograms overweight. I was lethargic and lacked motivation to eat well and get my body moving. It all seemed too hard.

Emotionally, I was self-sabotaging my thoughts and behaviours. This affected my relationship with food and grew into an eating disorder where I would overeat or else eat too little and then binge. I would eat healthy in public and binge on fast food as a means to control my emotions and unpleasant thoughts.

I was in an emotionally unhealthy relationship for 24 years. This reduced my self-esteem to the point I lost all self-worth and struggled with my identity. Sure, I was a wife, mother, boss, caregiver, sister and daughter, but didn't know who I was or what I stood for. What were my highest values, dreams and aspirations? Feelings of fear, rejection, "not good enough", unworthy, unlovable and regret dictated my life and thoughts.

Spiritually, I felt disconnected from God and as a result was disconnected from myself and this harmed my relationship with myself and others. I became socially isolated and withdrawn, overwhelmed with the feeling of loneliness.

> *The human journey is the same:*
> *face the shadow and move towards the light.*
> *The shadow will create the foundation*
> *to pursue the light.*

CHAPTER 1: MY JOURNEY

It was then I hit rock bottom in a desperate situation of do or die. My knees hit the ground and in total despair I surrendered all that I was to Jesus and asked for his forgiveness. I prayed for salvation, healing and restoration of my life.

Something profound happened to me that day. In fact, it was extraordinary. I was overwhelmed with pristine clarity, purpose, and direction like never before. I made a decision there and then to transform my life holistically. A journey within was born.

I set about making small changes in lifestyle, including my nutritional intake and getting my body moving. My exercise and nutrition evolved over time. Today I am exercising smarter to achieve optimal results and my nutrition is based primarily around clean eating using fresh and simple ingredients. Maintaining health and wellness doesn't have to be complicated and there is no one-size-fits-all method. It is important to find out what works for you and fits into your busy lifestyle.

So it was not until I addressed my *mindset* that I could be emotionally free to find my passion for life and live gratefully. My goal is emotional and spiritual wellbeing. Mindset is more powerful than most people realise and has the capacity to distort our perception of reality and ultimately sabotage our potential.

Perspective that is framed in truth—God's truth—is essential for each of us to be at our personal best physically, emotionally, and spiritually. God has the power to heal you physically, emotionally and socially and will restore you back to belonging, back to your community, including your family and friends.

Throughout my journey of transformation, I found it difficult to find support and motivation. Education was one of the major components that was lacking. My strong desire is to inspire and help transform people's lives through education, inspiration and support.

My vision is to help women and men experience awareness about the importance of a healthy mind and healthy lifestyle and their benefits as part of a journey of change and self-discovery.

Sometimes when it appears that things are falling apart, stop! Consider they may actually be falling into place. My journey within has helped me to rediscover the amazing power and peacefulness of living with a grateful heart.

BEAUTY BEHIND EVERY TEAR YOU CRY

I wrote the poem, wich you will read on the next page, to give me strength and encouragement during difficult times. I hope it gives you as much as it has given me.

There is beauty behind every tear you cry.
A heart that's beating at the speed of light,
A soul that's yearning love, peace and happiness.
Let your eyes show your fight
When you're stuck in a moment
And your spark has been stolen.
There is beauty behind every tear you cry.
Sometimes it's hard to realign.
Pray that lump in your throat is benign.
You've been waiting for that feeling all your life.
Know, trust, believe for a world that is rife.
Have hope for new beginnings,
For the storm will pass.
There is beauty behind every tear you cry.

CHAPTER 2

. . .

SELF WORTH

Usually when we think of love, we consider *romantic* love, God's *unconditional* love and *friendships*. We often miss the importance of *family affection*. This is the most basic of all loves, but it is too often taken for granted in our busy, hectic schedules. At times it is easy to become disconnected as a family. Family affection is a humble and soft love that ignores all barriers.

Tips to foster family affection:

* *Closeness without conformity.*

We often don't want people we love to change because we feel threatened that change will affect our closeness. The lesson is to appreciate and value your differences.

* *Ease without discourtesy.*

Ease needs to be combined with treating each family member with respect. The lesson is to enhance the ability to express feelings without the need to filter.

* *Sacrifice without expectation.*

Sometimes as parents we sacrifice for our children but expect a lifetime of gratitude and payback. Or sometimes children have a sense of entitlement from their parents. The lesson is that grace has no strings attached.

* *Hospitality without anxiety.*

People take you as they find you—authentic. The lesson is don't wait until your life is perfect to invite people into it. Be present now.

* *Service without resentment.*

As women we try to take on the world and be all things to everyone. The lesson is to ask for and accept help. Do not lose your identity or voice in your relationship. If you are a man allow your vulnerability to show. This is a profound strength within that builds bridges to your partner and family and ultimately back to you.

CHAPTER 2: SELF WORTH

> *Relationships are not an obligation.*
> *They are not duties, tasks or matters*
> *to be crossed off a list.*
> *You cannot have a relationship with someone*
> *because of a relationship they have had*
> *with someone else in your life.*
> *Relationships are a heart connection*
> *and require you to encounter people one by one!*

GOD'S UNCONDITIONAL LOVE

God is love and God's love is unconditional. The gospel message is a story of divine rescue, a gracious act of self-sacrifice. The focus of God's love is redemption.

> *"For by grace you have been saved through faith. And this is not your own doing, it is the gift of God."*
>
> —Ephesians 2:8 (ESV)

God's love is unlike a love expressed by many in society, a love of convenience and ego. His unconditional love is inspired by salvation, a healing of our soul, bringing us back to wholeness.

Speak the truth of God's love above all else. It matters not who you are, your circumstances, nor what you have done. God loves you. Rest in the arms of our Lord, and your soul will be restored, your life will be redeemed, and your future will have a hope like never before.

ROMANTIC LOVE

Romantic love is a powerful way to express uniquely our capacity to love and be loved.

The ingredients for long-lasting romantic love include friendship, respect, freedom, and transparency. As a human race we have a profound longing for connection where we feel comfortable baring our soul of who we really are. And in the process, we feel love, acceptance and security.

Marriage itself does not necessarily create or sustain romantic love. To love someone and for that to endure requires much

CHAPTER 2: SELF WORTH

"

A legacy is not in the things you leave
for people but in what you leave IN people.
Of hope and courage inscribed into their minds
and of a love carved deep into their hearts.

more than the institution of marriage itself. It requires that lessons be learnt and embraced. Consider the following statements:

- Love is the ability to see your partner with clarity. Fall in love with the real person, not your ideal of who you want that one to be.

- Love is communicating with ease. Love does not automatically teach communication skills. Work on these skills.

- Love is visible (desire to be seen). Express your own personality and values. Authenticity is essential.

- Love is unconditional. Be willing to do something together without expectation, control or fear.

- Love is vulnerable and raw. Be willing to make an emotional investment.

Believe in romance. Love is a profound mystery and unravelling this mystery can be magical and freeing as it takes courage to unravel that mystery called love.

FRIENDSHIPS

Aristotle declared friendship is a single soul dwelling in two bodies. It is the most unselfish of all loves as it is based on a genuine care and seeks only happiness and the best for each other.

Genuine friendship provides an anchor in an uncertain and ever-changing world. True friendship is unconditional. It is reciprocal. True friends accept each other's differences but also share commonalities.

The true meaning of friendship is when you consider the other person's well-being to be as valuable as your own. A true friend resides in your heart, not just in your mind.

CHAPTER 2: SELF WORTH

❝

*Give yourself permission
to communicate
what matters to you.*

Sometimes friendships can change as people change and their circumstances change. Along our journey we evolve, grow, and as a result our interests, goals, and desires will change. It is not unreasonable to think that our friendships will change.

However, some friends last a lifetime, and these are indeed precious. Time does not lessen a true friend's affinity for you. These relationships are based on mutual trust, respect and admiration.

A true friend is one who does not necessarily just accept you for who you are but supports you and encourages you to be a better version of yourself. True friends are a gift from God.

HAPPINESS

Happiness is not something that can be bought, consumed, acquired, worn or accumulated. It does not depend on gender, status, or wealth. It is intrinsic. The amazing thing is happiness is not something we need to wait for. It's available right here, right *now*. Tap into it!

Happiness is the spiritual experience of living every minute with love, grace and gratitude. Live gratefully and shine from within.

TRUTH IS YOUR COMPASS HOME

The challenge is our view of truth is sometimes distorted as it is tied to our perception of what others will think and to cultural perspective.

Truth may vary according to circumstances and opinions. Its definition is open to interpretation based on our beliefs, values, and experiences. Truth transcends culture and society's expectations. As we speak truth, we discover something greater than ourselves. God is truth, the absolute and true essence of being and reality, the author of all truth. Seek truth beyond yourself and you will be set free.

*Being at peace with those around you
doesn't mean you have to agree
with everyone all of the time.
It means you are tolerant, considerate
and gracious even when you don't agree.
There is a profound strength that comes to you
when you choose to walk in love: you live in peace.*

The spirit of truth is:

- Not always what makes people feel good;
- Not always what the majority say is true;
- Not always what appears coherent and easy;
- Not always comfortable and can be confronting or painful;
- Not made in error or deceptive;
- That which is *your* reality;
- Speaking up even if it means standing alone;
- Not fearing judgement;
- Being congruent with who you are and what you stand for;
- Your compass home, a connection to your heart.

ONE OF A KIND — YES, THAT'S YOU!

Are you wanting to shed your individuality to fit in? If so, you are robbing the world of the amazing person you are. Embrace who you are and know that you are extraordinary.

We tend to want to conform to what society tells us: one size fits all. We are neither taught nor encouraged to embrace who we are and celebrate our differences. For fear of being judged or discriminated against, we desire so much to be one of the crowd.

The perception of beauty is unique and different for each of us. Don't compare yourself to the unattainable concept of perfection you see in magazines. Often photos of models are airbrushed and adjusted to present snapshots of moments in time. They don't reflect who those models are or how they feel on the inside.

*Do not judge others
for being vulnerable
because one day you too will be there
in some shape or form.
Perfectly imperfect.*

It is not possible to be someone else. You were not designed that way. You were designed to be *you*. Learning to accept the way you see yourself is the most significant thing you can do for yourself. Love the way you look: short, tall, skinny, curvy, brunette, blonde, freckled, dimpled. Your style may evolve over time, but it's *your* style—have the courage to be an individual.

Know you are beautiful just as you are. Own it and celebrate it, not in an arrogant way, but in a humble and graceful way. Accept a compliment when someone tells you: *You look beautiful, I like your dress,* or *you have nice hair*. We often struggle to accept people's kindness and compliments as we judge ourselves harsher than others do.

Release yourself to express yourself in your unique way. Live as intentionally as possible. You were not meant to look like or behave like anyone else. You are one of a kind—God's masterpiece!

HAVE YOU LOST YOURSELF IN MOTHERHOOD, MARRIAGE AND CAREER?

Often in the pursuit of being the perfect mother, the perfect wife, the higher achiever, we lose our own identity. It is the result of the admirable quality of wanting to give everything to our children, our relationship and our career.

However, in this process we sometimes forget to be kind to ourselves and we lose track of what *we* believe in, what *we* stand for and what makes *us* happy. By ignoring our passions and interests, we lose our authenticity. This harms our health, vitality and wellness.

When was the last time you took time out for yourself and didn't feel guilty? If right now you feel depleted and unfulfilled, return inward and connect with your inner child. Revive your childhood dreams, spirit, and passion for life.

Our identity cannot be assumed or faked but emerges from within when we have the courage to step up and stand in our truth.

CHAPTER 2: SELF WORTH

❝

*You inspire others
to treat you by the way you treat yourself.
If you want love, respect, honesty,
forgiveness, compassion, and trust,
give these things to yourself first
and all else will follow.*

A woman who likes herself, knows herself, and respects herself enough to live an authentic life is already the amazing mother, wife, and success that she aspires to be.

YOUR VALUE IS INTRINSIC: YOU WERE BORN WITH IT

Your value does not depend on your heritage, the suburb you live in, your body type, your hair style, what clothes you wear, your job, your level of education, how many friends you have, who you know, the type of car you drive, or how big your house is.

You are valuable for who you are—the authentic *you*.

Ask yourself these questions:

- Where do I place my value?

- What do I say that matters to me?

Take care what you say to yourself because *you are listening*. Remind yourself each and every day you need to believe what you say and think matters.

If you are constantly trying to prove your worth to others, you have already forgotten it. Your value doesn't decrease because of someone's inability to see it. That's their issue. No matter what has happened in your life, what storm you have been through, or what your present situation is, your value never changes. You are a precious diamond, my dear friend. Know that you are valuable and celebrate that today and every day.

BEAUTY STARTS ON THE INSIDE

Beauty is not about being flawless or perfect, having a bikini body or being a fashion icon. Appearances can be deceiving. Beauty

CHAPTER 2: SELF WORTH

"

Your heart deserves the best gift from you.
It is asking you to listen to its whispers
and observe its language
in the form of your feelings.
Whom your heart chooses to love,
your life's work
and your purpose
all reside in your heart.

is about being your authentic self. Be comfortable and confident with who you are and what you stand for. Your beauty radiates through your wonderful smile, your thoughtful actions, your compassion, your generosity, your humility and your *love*.

When we shine from within, we are beautiful on the inside and out as nothing is more attractive than being our natural self—the way we are!

A CONFIDENT WOMAN: PERCEPTION VERSUS REALITY

Confidence:

It is not something we are born with or can be taught in a workshop. Rather it grows organically from within.

It is not about being the prettiest, smartest, or most successful, or having a supermodel body.

It is not about being arrogant, aggressive or unapproachable. Confidence is having grace.

Those who radiate a natural confidence are those you love to be around because they are compassionate, authentic and humble. A confident woman is herself and lives her life with a purpose and conviction irrespective of who agrees or disagrees with her.

Growing up, I had a much different perspective of what I thought confidence is all about. I have learnt it is precisely at the point that you *stop* trying to appear confident or caring what others think that you are indeed confident and become an amazing role model for those around you.

Consider these initiatives to bring about your natural confidence:

- Live your purpose. Be the authentic *you*.

> *We spend our lives
> trying to live up to others' expectations
> of who we are meant to be.
> This is a betrayal of your inner truth.
> Who you really are
> is not defined by the external world
> but by your internal sanctuary.*

- Accept your imperfections. They are your perfections.
- Recover from setbacks. Refuse to live in fear.
- Do not conform, avoid comparisons, be unique.
- Be open to love. You are loved and capable of loving.
- Own your feelings. Speak truth.
- Make a difference in the lives of others.

My hope is to encourage, support and inspire others to live an amazing life of purpose and conviction as together we can truly make a difference in this world.

YOU ARE THE FAIRYTALE STORY

It's every girl's dream and hope her foot fits the glass slipper and her dreams come true.

Dreams *do* come true and you can have anything in life if you let go of your fear, judgement, anxiety, stress and everything else that doesn't help you. Step out of your comfort zone, make a change, stand in your truth, follow your heart and above all have *faith*.

Life itself is the most wonderful fairy tale. Find that magic place in your heart and live from within there. When all our thoughts and actions stem from a place of compassion, grace and humility, magic happens.

Your relationship with yourself and with others will improve and this affects all aspects of your life in the most amazing way. You will then see the beautiful fairy tale you already live in.

God has the power to rescue, restore, and renew your life.

"

Comfort and nourish their hearts,
yet do not shackle them.
You may share your experiences,
yet do not impose your truth.
Love and nurture your children,
yet do not house their soul.

TRUE FRIENDS

Sometimes in life that one special friend comes along that you have an amazing soul connection with. You know the ones I'm talking about. They walk the journey of life with you, edify you and at times even carry you during your darkest hours. Hold these true friends dear to your heart for they are precious gifts from God.

WHAT IS SELF-LOVE?

Self-love is the simplicity of our inner beauty. It is dynamic and it grows from within.

Self-love is the appreciation for oneself that grows from taking actions that support our physical, emotional and spiritual growth. It is not a feel-good experience like buying a new dress or having a makeover or reading an inspirational book, though these are lovely experiences.

Self-love is within the actions we take that strengthen us. In the process we learn to accept our weaknesses are indeed our strengths, our imperfections become our perfections and we accept ourselves for who we are.

We stop self-sabotaging beliefs, learn to have compassion for ourselves and others and live a life filled with purpose and values.

Whatever the scenario, your story—your experience, your journey—is valuable. You are amazing and have the capacity to make a difference in the world.

RELATIONSHIPS: YOUR POSTURE OF LOVE

Irrespective of what season you are in presently—single, married, separated, widowed, divorced, heartbroken, or in a relationship—lean in.

CHAPTER 2: SELF WORTH

❝

*Parenting is an art,
and artists always work within polarities.
The miracle in parenting
is in knowing when to hold them close
and when to give them wings to soar.
And because parenting exists
within an inherently sophisticated
yet simplistic art form,
it requires even more conscious awareness
to reconcile and mediate these opposites.
These paradoxes are transcended
by conscious parenting.*

As a human race, we have a deep need to have intimate human contact — the kind where we feel comfortable to bare our souls of who we are and feel no shame in that and in the process to feel love, acceptance and security.

Relationships are great vehicles in the journey of life. However, know you don't have to be in a relationship to be complete. Your relationship status does not define you. Don't put your life on hold waiting for that to happen. Don't be wishing you were somewhere else. You are where you should be. Choose to live where you are right now and get on with your life.

Love is patient and kind. It is not angry, frustrating, demanding, controlling. Love has ingredients and they will be different for each relationship. Find out what they are for your relationship to build love. An ingredient necessary to any relationship is security and feeling safe. It is like the flour in the cake batter that holds it all together.

Relationships require willingness to:

- Do something together without expectation;

- Love unconditionally;

- Be vulnerable;

- Make emotional investment;

- Allow yourself to be seen.

Love is a profound mystery. Love is transient as there is no certainty in any relationship except God's intimate relationship with you. What there is, is an unravelling mystery that is magical, freeing and accepting. It takes courage to unravel that mystery which is *love*.

> *You can only be controlled by what you fear.*
> *Nothing else can control you.*
> *When you live from a place of love,*
> *the need to control or to be controlled dissipates.*
> *Love frees you.*

TRUE FRIENDSHIPS

Respect yourself enough to question and if necessary, to walk away from certain toxic situations or friendships, from anyone or any *thing* that does not value you for who you are or allow you to stand in your truth. More importantly, hold your true friends close to your heart, for they are precious gifts from God. True friends are like angels. They will lift you up when you have trouble flying.

True friends...

- Make you feel safe and will never judge you;

- Don't care what others think of you;

- See your pain when others believe your smile;

- Say good things behind your back and always speak truth to you, even though you may not want to hear it;

- Are like stars: You may not always see them, but you know they are there;

- Value you, allow you to stand in your truth, and don't want to change you;

- Walk in when everyone else walks out;

- Are a blessing.

CHAPTER 3

. . .

STRENGTH

EMOTIONAL PAIN: ACCEPTANCE

Often, we see pain as a negative experience; it absolutely can be such. Irrespective of your circumstances, the pain can be debilitating, limiting, isolating and can instil fear and cause you to lose hope.

However, I put to you that you have the power of *choice*. You can either let that pain define you by choosing to stay in it, or choose to adjust and learn from the experience and in doing so catapult forward into amazing things.

Pain can be a great indicator of what is going on deeper inside you. Often, when we choose to ignore it or mask it, it manifests itself in an unhealthy situation. It is important to understand the pain you are feeling in order to be able to move past it.

So, make a *shift*: look at pain as a catalyst for change and consider these positive associations and thoughts: breakthrough, exploration of vulnerability, gratitude for good times, empathy for others, resilience, growth and strength, life experience, authenticity.

Nothing in life has the power to define who you are and determine who you will be. Do not give power to people or circumstances to determine your future. Let your story bleed into something more beautiful than regret, resentment and isolation.

Build resilience and choose to live out of joy, peace and conviction that brings light, hope, and inspiration to others.

EMOTIONAL PAIN: RESILIENCE

Resilience is not something you're either born with or not. It's not something that can be bought, sold or taught in a workshop. Rather it develops organically from within as we grow and gain better self-management skills, knowledge, and understanding of who we are and what we stand for.

> *Where there is light there is darkness*
> *and just as the sun rises at dawn, the sun sets at dusk.*
> *So too, where there is joy there is sorrow.*
> *For how can you truly know the feeling of joy*
> *if you have not experienced the pain of sorrow?*

Our life journey and circumstances allow us to individually grow and learn to become stronger and better able to cope with challenges in the future.

Resilience can be enhanced by cultivating the right environment, including relationships with others, cultural beliefs and society. This is where our thoughts, beliefs and actions that lessen our ability to be resilient are learned and developed.

Make good choices of who or what you allow in your inner circle of influence.

A resilient person will:

- Admit and embrace vulnerability;
- Seek and ask for help;
- Find manageable parts to a problem;
- Develop the ability to say no;
- Set healthy boundaries;
- Use their power to make a choice;
- Turn resentment into forgiving;
- Find meaning in their difficulty;
- Walk away from unhealthy situations and relationships;
- Be able to stand alone when needed.

THE POWER OF CHOICE: OWN IT!

Expect at some stage in life you will encounter crossroads, defining moments that will require you to make a choice. They will

CHAPTER 3: STRENGTH

❝

*There will come a point when your change is so resilient,
no one can make you doubt yourself
and your setbacks become minor diversions.
You stop being influenced by other people's control
dramas and more importantly your own.*

test you and make you feel uncomfortable or even downright petrified.

One road will require you to make a choice that takes courage, strength and tenacious faith. This road is challenging but will open up an amazing future and hope like never before.

The other road is a continuation of what you know and have experienced already. Don't choose this road simply because you prefer to stay in the safety of your comfort zone. These choices can be limiting—restrictive—and can result in living without purpose and meaning.

Choices can be influenced by culture and people who love you. Don't give that power away to others. Personal power comes with the decisions you make.

Next time you come to a tough choice, reflect on the defining moments you've already experienced and the lessons you've learnt. Also consider these points about what is important:

- It's not what happened in your life, it's what you do now.
- It's not always about the opportunities. Work with what you have.
- It's not who you are, it's who you become.
- You are wired for *love*. Make good choices.

TREE OF LIFE AND LOVE

As women we have beautiful, endearing qualities. We show love and compassion towards others, we know how to pick the perfect greeting cards, we cry at the movies, we hold our dear friends close to our hearts and we love to play peacemaker.

Yet, we have trouble showing that same level of love and respect to ourselves. Sometimes we hold ourselves back from giving our hearts completely. Why? Is it fear that our heart will be broken or

CHAPTER 3: STRENGTH

❝

*The human heart,
so delicately fragile yet profoundly strong and resilient.
And so this is the miracle itself,
that the human heart becomes stronger
only after its been broken.*

rejected? Sometimes our hearts are indeed stubborn or filled with anger such that we find it difficult to forgive our past.

Begin your heart makeover and renew your thoughts today. Your thoughts are like trees: they expand and grow branches. Don't be a victim of words spoken over you or your past. Choose your thoughts as they will grow your roots, which in turn will grow your branches. Choose to grow healthy branches. Don't grow a thorny black tree. Grow a luscious, green, leafy tree full of life and love.

LIONESS ARISING

Is your greatest fear in the world what the opinion of others is about you?

The moment you are unafraid of the crowds, you become a lioness.

Awaken your untamed nature, your fierce beauty and your unbridled strength.

You are allowed to have an opinion.

You are allowed to have a voice.

You are allowed to have a vision.

Pursue that dream with passion and a renewed strength.

And as you do, a great roar arises in your heart: the roar of freedom and your truth.

DON'T UNDERESTIMATE YOUR COURAGE

Courage is *truth* in its most pure and fragile form. Courage is not arrogance or ego but displays humility and grace. No matter what

>

The challenge is to gracefully balance and flow with ease between your compassionate vulnerability and your compassionate strength, that you may be a warrior and yet a defender of peace.

your pain, anger, bitterness, guilt, fear, grief, regret, or shame, it takes courage to let go of the past.

Courage speaks the truth of God's love. It gives us beauty for our ashes and this love has the ability to redeem our future and give us a hope like never before as we experience a renewed strength and vision of power and authority.

Go on a journey to discover what courage means to you.

Courage to:

- Be vulnerable;
- Accept your imperfections;
- Say *I love you* when you look in the mirror;
- Take time out for yourself and not feel guilty;
- Say I am worthy and capable;
- Find your voice and speak your truth;
- Overcome personal challenges;
- Ask for help;
- Forgive yourself and others;
- Go after your dreams;
- Be yourself;
- Embark on a health and wellness journey;
- Say no and yes;
- Let your light shine and be amazing.

CHAPTER 3: STRENGTH

>

*In a world that prefers you
to follow the "norm" and be the status quo;
avoid it at all costs.
Rise against the torrential waves
of societal expectation and conformity
with every fibre of who you are
and who you choose to be.
Do all you can to avoid
being the industry standard,
for even the highest industry standard
is mundane.*

IN THE MIDST OF DARKNESS YOUR LIGHT WILL PREVAIL

Are you travelling through life within safe parameters, seeking ease and staying within your comfort zone? If frustration is missing from your life, this may be an indication you have chosen the path of least resistance, of least challenges and therefore of least growth, for you experience the most growth in the valleys when you stretch and lengthen yourself beyond what you already know.

If you are going through a difficult time right now, remember you are not alone. Sometimes it may feel like you are alone, but trust that God knows exactly where you are and what is your breaking point.

Right now, you may be in the midst of darkness. It may be due to financial pressures, relationships, health matters, career decisions, addiction, toxic body and food relationships, or unhealthy lifestyle. Irrespective what your personal situation is, this is when the Lord says: "Take courage. It is I. Don't be afraid." Sometimes the frustrations of life will try to blind you to His presence. Have faith and never lose sight of the amazing love He has for you and your future.

Make a decision today to step out of your comfort zone, out of the realm of the natural and into the supernatural, as this is where miracles happen. Holding onto your faith in the middle of your frustration can bring the greatest miracle of all.

NEVER EVER, EVER GIVE UP

Storms in life can cause fear and uncertainty and can shake your foundation to its core. Sometimes the storm seems incomprehensible: loss of finances, loss of job, loss of security, relationship breakdowns, illness, or death of loved ones.

Maybe you feel helpless today and are in despair. Maybe you are in a dark place, overwhelmed by the situation you are facing and wondering when and if it will ever get better.

CHAPTER 3: STRENGTH

❝

*You cannot give up merely
because a situation doesn't seem ideal.
No you cannot!
You are beautiful in your imperfection,
outrageously courageous in your doubts,
lovable even in your feelings
of unlovability and sturdy
in the moments when you stumble.
There is no self to change,
no self to defend
and no self to make perfect.
Let go of every impossible ideal.
All these parts have been given;
all are parts of the whole
and you are complete.*

The following passage has helped me through many dark times:

> "But those who trust in the Lord for help will find their strength renewed. They will rise on wings like eagles; they will run and not get weary; they will walk and not grow weak."
>
> —Isaiah 40:31

Your storm will pass, and your faith in something greater than what's seen with your eyes can restore your life, whether you call that God, a higher power, universal energy or something else. Never, ever, ever give up!

WHATEVER YOUR SEASON, YOU'RE NOT ALONE

Statistics regarding loneliness have never been so high. "Me time" is healthy and a necessary part of life. I'm talking about the feeling of being forsaken, abandoned, lonely and misunderstood. We are more connected than ever with technology, yet we are more disconnected than ever.

Have you retreated or isolated yourself because of your difficult circumstances? Most people think because they have baggage or are facing a difficult season, they need to run away for fear of judgement. It's a natural response. If you feel your situation is inflexible, whatever that might be for you, this is the time to run towards true friendships. True friends will not judge you because Jesus does not judge you.

Retreating from relationships or from community is not healthy. In fact, isolation can get you into big trouble. It often leads to negative thoughts and irrational decisions because when you are alone, you can justify everything. It all makes sense to you.

"

*Never assume
you are stuck with the way things are right now.
Your life is a direct result
of the choices you have made and will make.
If you don't like where you are,
it's time to make a different choice.*

Too many people are suffering, feeling isolated and disconnected. If you know people like this, here is a call on you to reach out to them. Show them you care about their life. People are looking for authentic relationships. True friends will carry each other in times of despair. True friends will walk the journey of life together. True friends will make a way when you feel there is no way. True friends will remove the limitations you have placed on yourself.

We were designed for friendships, community, and relationships. Declare to someone that they never have to be alone. You are the seed or missing piece of the puzzle. Keep serving, loving, caring, and offering. You don't have to try to-do anything more. God is the orchestrator.

If right now you have baggage, have made mistakes, or are wondering and searching, reconnect with community. Jesus knows the power of belonging and community. He heals people physically, emotionally and socially. It's the most wonderful revelation of the Shepherd's heart.

THE PERSON BEHIND THE MASK

A mask is a beautiful fantasy, but life is not an ongoing masquerade ball. Most of us wear a kind of mask, a persona that hides our deepest thoughts and feelings. We present a confident, polished, rehearsed, controlled face to the world.

Have you chosen to wear a mask and hide your true self for fear of rejection, judgement or vulnerability? Do you hide your emotions to avoid drama? Do you put up barriers to protect yourself? The problem is when you do this for too long, you soon forget your true self.

Let people in to see the person behind the mask, the person behind the eyes. It can be unnerving but also wonderful. We all long to be seen and to be known, which is nourishing to the soul. I

CHAPTER 3: STRENGTH

❝

Strength comes from vulnerability.
From allowing oneself to experience feelings
rather than hide them
or hide from them.

know you long to have your hopes and feelings acknowledged—the ones behind your polite, orchestrated smile. Most intimately, you (like everyone else) long for your innermost being to be recognised by someone and accepted for what it is.

This requires you to look deeper than what can be seen on the surface: the pretty face, nice body, wealth, status, fashion and so forth. Focus on the love shining through the person's eyes and warming your heart.

This week, get a sense of the person behind the eyes of those around you. Don't get distracted by surface details. Let recognition of the person show in your face, in your own eyes. Be brave. Get to know someone for real and allow someone to get to know you for real.

Watch how this process changes the course of interaction, softening it and making it more authentic. We can know people without *really* knowing them. You may think that you know who you are, but maybe you are wrong because who you are is what others tell you to be. Take time to rediscover your true self beneath your mask and the people around you. Transform relationships.

WHAT DID YOU DO FOR SOMEONE ELSE TODAY?

Have you happily given someone some of your time? Have a coffee together? Comfort them in time of need? Give them a hug? Call and check on a friend you haven't heard from for a while? Send someone a special card showing them you're thinking of them? Tell someone you appreciate them?

Sometimes even little words need to be spoken; just being there is enough. These things don't cost money but can make a profound impression when we help from the heart.

> *A lightness of heart
> brings a lightness of heart.
> Perception is your reality.*

SORRY!
JUST ANOTHER WORD IN OUR VOCABULARY?

True meaning is reflected in the conviction behind what you say. Heartfelt apologies can go a long way, encouraging forgiveness and mending a broken heart.

Too often we think of how others have done us wrong, hurt us, manipulated us, or taken advantage of our generous heart. But how often have you thought about the pain you may have caused someone else?

We often find it difficult to apologize. This is because we tend to view apologies as a sign of weak character. Popular culture tells us we need to "win" and this quest for perfection is tied to our pride and ego.

It is absolutely scary to expose your vulnerability to the possibility of rejection. But don't just stand firm in your resolve, justifying your actions with self-serving biases for this reason alone. We often manage our emotions in an effort to protect our fragile sense of self as we feel more comfortable with anger, frustration and disappointment compared to confronting vulnerability.

A genuine apology offered and accepted is one of the most profound gifts you can give and receive. It has the power to generate forgiveness and restore damaged relationships. In the process it builds greater trust, respect and love for the other party. It takes great strength to say *sorry* and admit your mistake.

Opening up in such a way requires humbling yourself. This process is empowering. If your actions or *in*actions have affected someone adversely, I urge you to call, write, or visit the affected one in person and have a beautiful conversation.

Sure, you put yourself out there for the possibility of rejection but that's how you learn and blossom and in the process, live by your values. One of the most difficult things to live with is having words to say in your heart but being too afraid to say them.

"

*A vibrant luminous light
continues to shine
where a beautiful soul has travelled.
Strength, courage and unconditional love
will endure.*

KNEEL IN THE DARK SO YOU CAN STAND IN THE DARK

If right now you have fallen, are in pain, have messed up your life, lost your job, failed in your relationship, lost a friend, or are facing trouble, kneel in this darkest hour so you can stand in the darkest places.

I'm referring to tenacious faith, where you humble yourself. Too many people in this world are standing up and shouting, wanting to be heard. It's not about having the loudest voice. Know who you are in Christ and let no one judge you or persecute you. Feed your faith, and then doubt, fear, rejection, abandonment and vulnerability will surrender as you expand in Love.

If the tides of life have turned against you and the current has swept you out to sea, don't flap around and struggle to swim. You will run out of puff. Instead, lie on your back and float in the arms of deep faith. Imagine knowing the full power of what it means to turn to God or universal energy. When you decide to kneel down, it changes you and you are made stronger and more resilient. This energy flows through you like never before.

Silence the distractions around you so you can hear what God has planned for your life. Stand for something so you won't fall for anything. Too many people just exist.

ARE YOU ON THE REGRET HIGHWAY?

Should've, could've and *would've* no longer suffice. So, you have made mistakes? Perhaps you haven't made the right career choice or followed your heart in love. Perhaps you've settled for less than what you deserve in your life. Or perhaps you've hurt others.

Irrespective of your circumstances, get off the highway of regret. Move on, learn, and grow from the past; know that now you will not settle for anything less than you deserve. Most importantly,

> *In some circumstances*
> *you "just can't imagine"*
> *how another person could*
> *"do such a thing",*
> *"say such a thing"*
> *and "act in such a way".*
> *In this moment you have simply forgotten*
> *where you came from*
> *and where both you and the other person*
> *are going.*
> *Collective consciousness awakening.*

don't make the same mistake twice because then it's no longer a mistake. It's a choice. Make a choice for a better life.

Don't be afraid, ashamed, or regretful of your past circumstances. Your best teacher is your last mistake. In every mistake there is a lesson to be learnt, but sometimes we miss the lesson because we are too caught up in being regretful. These lessons are meant to guide you, but they do not define you.

Actually, let's not even think of it as a mistake. Let's refer to it as a detour in life. These are events that have happened that allow you to learn and grow in order to reach the places you want to go. Real success is about moving forward despite the mistakes you've made.

So, get out there and give it a go. You'll only regret the chances you didn't take, relationships you were afraid to have and decisions you wanted to make but didn't. The most significant opportunities are found from lessons learnt in times of difficulty. Never regret anything that has happened in your life.

Choose to make a better choice.

IT'S YOUR TIME TO FLY

We can use the analogy of the metamorphosis of the caterpillar into a butterfly in our own lives. Irrespective of where you presently are in your life, discover your divine purpose and what is authentic to you. Perhaps you feel cocooned in your world and merely focus on just getting through the day.

Do you think only of survival and your immediate needs, like a restricted caterpillar who doesn't realise that anything else is possible? Alter your thoughts, choose love and light and in the process, you will attract these vibrations from others. Tap into your inner source, God's love for you and let your heart speak.

CHAPTER 3: STRENGTH

❝

*Vulnerability
is the Universal language
that everyone understands!*

If you feel you are living in a toxic cocoon of negative emotions, thoughts, or other people's expectations, let go of what you know and step into the unknown. Don't let your lack of experience and difficult circumstances restrict you and have you thinking that living a life of your dreams is not possible. Make your own choices to achieve a different result.

The caterpillar also thinks what it knows is all there is to know, but as a butterfly it sees the true beauty of the world and the bigger picture. The butterfly has a different imprint and purpose, which is to pollinate plants and continue the creation of life. Your blueprint of potential is already within you and your cocoon of change is unique to you. Don t compare. Let your eternal nature emerge. It is a form of knowledge innately within you.

I urge you to be the butterfly you already are. Gently, compassionately, and lovingly let go of the self-doubt, blame, fear and judgement. You already are what you want to become. Step out of the comfort of your cocoon. Readjust your perceptions of who you are and think you are and be patient in the process.

You are a beautiful butterfly, present and already in form. It's your time to fly.

BE STILL: FIND YOUR *BEING-NESS*

Give yourself permission to escape. Be still to find *being-ness*. When you are in this space, you return to "thyself." It is a transcending experience of the physical and emotional dimensions into an experience of your true nature. It feels different. There is a sense of choice as you remove personality, gender, age, ethnicity and culture. Peel back the opinions brought on by social and cultural conditioning. In this process you are transcending all things physical, mental and psychological.

When your mind is completely silent and your body is completely still, you have regressed to a point of profound silence and

> *Everything in life is impermanent.
> So when things are going good
> be grateful for all things good
> as season's do and will change.
> It also means that
> when life becomes challenging,
> that season shall too pass.
> Be grateful for the stretch,
> the wisdom and growth
> you've experienced.*

stillness. What you are left with is a point of being-ness and connection to your soul as you move into an internal silence. In that emptiness your awareness remains pure light of consciousness to the source: God and the universe.

In the midst of chaos, pain and difficult circumstances, take time to silence your mind and body because your thoughts and what's going on around you can be distracting and self-defeating. This process can have a profound effect on the way you think over time because our thoughts precede our actions and determine choice and quality of life.

EMPOWERMENT: THE NEW AGE BUZZWORD

In today's society we hear the word *empowered* used often. There are many courses, seminars, retreats on how to become empowered and how to empower others. However, it is not something that can be taught, learnt, or passed on to someone else. I do believe, however, it is possible to help a person to discover their own feeling of empowerment that already lies within them.

Feeling empowered is not a skill that can be taught but rather a process of our journey of self-discovery and making a deliberate choice to live out of joy, peace, conviction and grace. By its own nature, living in this way empowers you and as a result brings hope and inspiration to others. Consider these qualities of an empowered man and woman.

An empowered man and woman believes:

- In their intrinsic value;

- They are wonderfully made yet imperfect;

- In their power of choice;

- In their ability of resilience;

CHAPTER 3: STRENGTH

❝

For anyone going through a tough time...
I know you've been hurt.
I know how it feels.
Believe me, I do,
but the feeling will ease,
the tears will stop falling
and your heart will begin to heal itself.
Love is way more powerful than fear
and will always bring you back home
to The Light.

- Their potential is limitless;

- They are one of a kind;

- In their dream and purpose.

Above all, an empowered man and woman is humble, graceful, compassionate, authentic, speaks truth and lives her life congruently with who they are and what they stand for. In other words, they "walks the talk" irrespective of the opinions of others.

THE HEALING POWER OF FORGIVING

Are you carrying a burden in your heart as a result of your past? Perhaps you've been hurt physically or emotionally, or have been abused, betrayed or abandoned. Your experience doesn't make sense to you and you feel despondent. While nothing can change or undo the past, you can do something about your present and future. Forgiving others, including yourself, makes a way for healing to begin.

Forgiveness does not for a minute justify or excuse the pain that you have experienced and is not always easy to do when you have been hurt at a deep level. At times, it feels more painful to forgive than the wound itself.

The endless rage, resentment, guilt and anger you may be feeling will drain the life out of everything you do. Forgiveness is an act of compassion, a state of grace. Find forgiveness in your heart for those who have hurt you and you will rise to a higher level of self-love and wellbeing. Forgiveness sets the prisoner free "you" and places you at cause and not effect of your life.

Forgiving others starts as a decision of surrender, an act of will. This surrender invites God and universal life force energy to begin working in your life and bring healing to you.

> *Happiness is a choice,*
> *Unhappiness is a choice.*
> *Always at each moment*
> *you have a choice.*

CHAPTER 3: STRENGTH

The healing power of forgiveness is the key to your peace, health and happiness.

Forgiveness heals your heart and frees it to love again.
Forgiveness restores your power.
Forgiveness doesn't change your past
but enhances your future.
Forgiveness sets the prisoner (you) free.

CHAPTER 4

．

．

．

PURPOSE

WHAT DO YOU WANT TO BE REMEMBERED FOR?

Wealth, achievement, fame? Live your life with purpose, empathy, grace, compassion and humility. Smile a lot and make someone happy. These are the actions that will make others remember you. It is precisely at the moment when you stop living your life for the sole purpose of wanting to be remembered that you leave a lasting legacy.

YOUR DREAM IS YOUR DESTINY

Dream...to live, to love, to make a difference! Live your life with a God-given dream, and in the process inspire vision in others. Where there is no vision, people live carelessly, aimlessly, without purpose and are often unfulfilled and risk perishing emotionally. Vision keeps you on purpose, on track for living an amazing life of passion, determination and true contribution in this world.

Often our environment will not encourage us to dream or pursue our passion. It may be frowned upon or even ridiculed. However, if you have a dream planted deep within your soul, I encourage you to pursue that dream like never before. Your dream will threaten some people, often the ones closest to you. Your dream may cause envy in people you love. It can come from the closest persons in life: family, colleagues, friends.

Remember these key points along your journey:

- Dreamers never stop dreaming. Your dream may be audacious but dare to dream. Dreamers keep dreaming and evolving. Anyone who loses their vision for the future will always return to the past.

- Dreamers understand other dreamers. Seek people that encourage and sharpen you. A diamond is the strongest natu-

"

Boundless love is expansive.
It is a love more comforting
than the warmth of a log fire.
It is more exquisite than the beauty of a smile
or the droplets of the misty rainfall.
More captivating than the scent of the blossoming rose
and more delightful than the taste of sweet love.

rally occurring material on earth. It can be cut only by another diamond. Seek other diamonds in your life.

You may feel like a speck in the universe, but *never* underestimate God and his plans for your dream.

Dream... to live, to love, to make a difference!

It takes the following three things to make your dream a reality:

- *A will to survive:* The life of a dreamer can be a lonely road as many will not understand your journey. There will be many distractions, discouragements and disappointments that will test you, including lack of resources and lack of support. Never, ever give up.

- *A will to succeed:* You have not been given a dream of mediocrity. No matter what inhibitions you have, if God has planted something deep within your heart, trust this energy to guide you into more truth.

- *A will to serve:* Every step of the way, serve faithfully. This requires compassion, humility, grace, empathy and a genuine love to help others and truly make a difference in this world. It is where we move away from "I" and "me" to "them" and "others".

Most people have the will to survive. It is a natural instinct. Fewer people have the will to succeed when it involves sacrifice, speaking truth or standing firm in their convictions, even if it means standing alone. Some people aren't prepared to walk this road and want success without paying the price. Even fewer people want or have the will to serve because the will to serve is selfless. The destiny of your dream is not only about you. It is about others.

Be alive to succeed and succeed in wanting to serve. Those who do are the one percent of people with a story to tell, a testimony to share. If your gift or dream is to serve others, you are the one percent. Make your dream a reality. You have been called to do so!

"

*Boundless love is expansive
whereby you are imbued by life itself,
bursting to bathe in its Mystery,
Magic and Secret Wisdom.
And with each breath and firing neuron,
you courageously pursue to discover
the boundless possibilities
that exist within you.*

HAPPINESS: IT'S ALL THAT MATTERS

If you have been thinking recently, *I just want to be happy*, take a moment right now to consider exactly what this means for you. Happiness is a state of the heart. It is when your life feels satisfied, content and as it should be in its natural flow. The key is to understand with clarity what you are wishing for. Then just do it.

THE RIVER FLOWS IN YOU

The journey of life isn't necessarily about finding yourself or what you are meant to do in your life. It's about learning to love and accept yourself for who you are. In the process these other things happen anyway.

Let there be no judgement, no fear, no shame, no guilt, no anger, no regret, no self-sabotaging thoughts, no frustration, no procrastination, no retaliation, no humiliation. Accept your imperfections and that indeed you are compassionate, humble and generous. In the process you will learn to be kind and forgiving to yourself and to others.

To be loved, open your heart to love. Choose to accept only the kind of love you greatly deserve. Don't settle for anything less. Love speaks many languages but it's the action behind the word that is universal.

Don't live a life without love for fear of rejection, judgement, or hurt. To love takes courage. A life without love is like a plant trying to grow without sunlight. Eventually it wilts and loses its will to thrive. To love is to forgive and to see imperfection as perfection in you and in others.

Love is like a boomerang. Sometimes you just have to throw it and see if it comes back to you. Love is a gentle action that speaks to and nourishes the soul of your heart. Let the river flow in you.

CHAPTER 4: PURPOSE

*Expansive love
is imbued in the essence of your being.
On every level,
in every cell of your body,
in every oxygen molecule in your breath
and firing neuron in your brain.*

ARE YOU WAITING FOR SOMETHING?

Is your life on pause until you get that perfect job, pay rise, promotion, perfect body, perfect partner, perfect family and more?

If right now you don't feel good about yourself, will achieving these things make you happy? I put to you and share from personal experience that it only masks the pain. When self-love is missing, our judgement becomes impaired and often we end up making not the best choices.

Stop waiting for tomorrow, next month, or next year, when you think you will have these things in order to be happy. All these things are wonderful to have but they do not bring you happiness if it doesn't already exist from within.

Stop waiting for someone to fall in love with you. Fall in love with yourself. No one can bring you happiness. However, someone else can help bring out something you already have: *love.*

Don't wait for someone to bring you flowers. Plant the seed of love in the garden of your soul and celebrate the beautiful person you are. Happiness is not something that can be bought or sold. Rejoice in who you already are and what you already have.

WHAT ON EARTH AM I HERE FOR?

Do you feel unfulfilled, empty, distracted, unsure, frightened, or even helpless? If so, you are not alone. Most people live their life searching.

God never intended for your spiritual journey to be unclear. Clarity about what you are to do, about your purpose becomes evident as you travel through your spiritual journey.

Love is your teacher...
It teaches compassion
It teaches trust
It teaches patience
It teaches forgiveness.

Here are four key things to remember as you do this:

- Your intimate relationship with God and universal life force energy fuels everything in your life.

- Open the eyes of your heart to experience enlightened freedom.

- Discover purpose and know the hope of your journey. There is a plan for your life.

- You are already standing on a mountain of value. Your story and experience are unique and valuable to this world.

As a human race our highest need is to know that we have made a difference in this world. Enjoy the riches of connecting with community, as together we can make a profound change. We all have different gifts. Maybe yours is just a little hidden at the moment and not obvious to you. Or is it clear but you are too afraid to own it and let it shine?

You have something in your life that comes easy, naturally, something that consumes your mind all the time and makes you beam a bright light at the thought of pursuing this dream. This seed of life and passion has been planted in your soul for a reason.

Make a decision not to be a spectator in your life. Run onto the field and play. Get together with the rest and share in the inheritance of together to make a real difference in this world. This is precisely the story of the journey.

OPEN YOUR HEART TO LOVE

The journey to love is a journey to finding your true self, your highest, most sacred and loving self. It's a love based on compassion, respect for life, acceptance of your past, grace and faith.

We are all capable of this love. Let go of the negative emotions of your past, ego and selfishness. Seek and you will find the essence

*Pay attention
to the things you are naturally drawn to:
what feeds your soul,
uplifts you and enlightens your being.
For these things
are mostly connected to your path,
passion and purpose in life.*

of who you really are. We need to love ourselves unconditionally in order to live gratefully and be able to love others. Forgive yourself, forgive others and show gratitude for your past, as that has shaped you for your tomorrow. Open your heart to love.

BOLDNESS IS YOUR CALLING

Being bold is risky and requires you to step out of your comfort zone. Are you sitting on a dream, a new idea or concept, or a career change but are afraid to speak your truth for fear of failure, rejection or criticism?

Boldness is a state of being. If you feel insecure, shy, timid, inferior or apprehensive, you are being called to be bold. The righteous are as bold as a lion. Don't be afraid of failing. What matters is taking a step out in faith and believing God will help you.

You were not designed to live downtrodden, restricted and in fear. You have been given a spirit of power. It is in your genetic makeup. Don't wait for momentary boldness to change your future, but rather know who you are in Christ and choose to live your life in boldness.

If you are afraid of making a mistake, let it go! True courage is displayed when you have made mistakes and are afraid, but you keep moving forward anyway. Boldness is a state of mind. Revisit what you are convinced of and make sure it's your truth and not what popular culture tells you to think. Don't be so afraid of being judged or failing that you stop following your dreams and merely float in limbo, not fulfilling your true potential. It's a huge injustice!

Consider how you will feel on the other side. Step out of your difficult circumstances, break free from the restrictions of your past and speak your truth. Consider how this will affect you and your ability to pursue the dreams in your heart, your friendships and

CHAPTER 4: PURPOSE

"

Pay attention...
When you really pay attention,
everything will become your teacher,
everything!

future relationships. Imagine what is on the other side waiting to be accomplished when you step out in boldness.

KNOWLEDGE IS ENLIGHTENMENT

Enlightenment is the transformation of our consciousness. It is the will that has to be engaged that allows you to transform yourself. Expand your consciousness to transcend the external being and become connected to the infinite source of light and wisdom, the universe and our Creator.

We are multidimensional beings made up of an energy complex. Our energy body is composed of layers of energy in which are embedded different types of consciousness. At the centre of all these layers is the way of the heart.

A joyful heart is a state of being-ness. This state is infectious and extends to others because the heart is what connects us all. The energy of love is universal and the most powerful of all. It cannot be defeated. This knowledge is power because it changes the way we think, the way we look at ourselves, and the way we relate to each other and to the world. We evolve.

DREAMS ARE CULTIVATED IN THE RIGHT ENVIRONMENT

Your dreams are your innermost secrets to your soul. Cultivating the right environment can be a difficult process but is essential if you are to live your dreams.

It can be difficult because over the years we have built up clutter in our minds such as unhealthy thoughts, self-sabotaging beliefs, or unhealthy relationships and we too often accept the opinion or seek the validation of others.

> *Love!*
> *You do not make yourself love.*
> *You surrender and allow love to become you.*
> *Real projection of loving energy*
> *has no attachment or intention.*
> *It just is.*
> *Divine beauty in it's most basic form.*

These negative environments make you believe you are not good enough, skilled enough, strong enough, fit enough, pretty enough, or smart enough and your fear sets in. Surrender your fears to cultivate the right environment.

It is an injustice if you are not pursuing the hopes and dreams that have been planted in you. You were designed with a purpose and have something special to offer the world.

EGO: AN ILLUSION OR REAL?

Your ego is an illusion that stands between you and the power of your intention. Why? Ego is fear-based. You focus on protecting yourself and your emotions in the interest of self-preservation. Your ego feeds your desire to be accepted, acknowledged, loved and valued.

Connecting to intention means listening to your heart and listening to your inner voice to discover who you are and what your purpose is. It is irrelevant what others think. If you are overly concerned with what others think, you have disconnected yourself from your intention because you have allowed the opinion of others to guide you. This is your ego at play.

Your ego is a collection of thoughts that you identify with. The problem is that ego is based on false identification. People tend to attach their worth to a person or thing or responsibility. So, when we lose our job, retire, or end a relationship, or when other significant changes occur in our life, we find it difficult to adjust. These triggers disrupt the cohesiveness of our ego and we tend to struggle with identity issues and finding balance again.

Your connections with others are absolutely essential. In fact, many of my posts encourage this point. However, the key is to connect with the real you rather than a distorted picture fuelled by your ego. Learn to transcend your ego, to experience true free-

CHAPTER 4: PURPOSE

LOVE
is the best medium of communication.
It provides a space for your truth
and the other person's truth.

dom and happiness that comes with being the authentic you and not trying to become someone with a certain image and constructed qualities.

Stay on purpose, detach from outcome, take responsibility for your choices and what resides *within*, the truest essence of your being.

BEING CALLED: STEP OUT IN FAITH

Don't be surprised when you feel called to step out in faith and do something you don't feel qualified to do. There is certainty within the higher power that you can do it long before you know how to do it. Whatever passion or dream has been planted in your heart, do not fear or have doubt. You are equipped and empowered by The King of kings.

When He calls you, He equips you. God doesn't always call the equipped; he equips the people he calls. Learn to lean on Him, for He will be your strength, your wisdom and your guidance. Choose wisely your environment—who and what you surround yourself with—as this will affect you.

Whatever has been put in your hands and heart has been put there for a reason. You have a purpose. Your mandate is to work on it so you can make it better. This will take time, energy and financial investment, so you must have patience. Ask for help and seek advice from experts, health professionals, coaches and practitioners to guide you, however, remember that only you truly have the keys to awaken your purpose for your life. You are a leader, a leader of your own life and everything you think, say, choose and action declares: "This is who I am and who I choose to be". Let go of the perpetual self-help hamster wheel. A gentle reminder that anything left unattended will deteriorate over time and you may soon realise that what you had is gone.

So, remember to "tender the garden in order to receive its fruits" which means to continue to work on what you already have, in-

CHAPTER 4: PURPOSE

"

*Consider for a moment... just one moment
the feeling of going beyond the obvious,
beyond what you know to be safe,
beyond what may seem logical
and the obvious choice.
Make still the chatter
and allow your imagination to create.
Now you soar high on wings of an eagle,
boundless, eternal and free.*

cluding your health and wellness, relationships, personal development, spiritual growth and career. So, if you want something, have courage, go for it, and never, ever, *ever* give up.

TO LOVE AND TO BE LOVED

Who or what we really are is love. We exist to love and be loved. The problem is when we turn this simple concept into a *need* to be loved and a *need* to love, which is fear-based rather than just being love.

Through the filter of the ego, sometimes the essence of being loved turns into the need for approval. The need to love others turns into a need for control.

In our lifetime we may experience both scenarios, but we usually gravitate towards one. We tend to attract partners with the opposite need. A person with a strong need for control will attract someone with a need for approval. As a result, we form the perfect approval and controlling dysfunctional relationship and exist in an illusion.

Let go of the need for control and allow others to make their own choices so they can accept consequences in their own life's journey. Let go of the need for approval and move towards alignment with your higher authentic self.

Love is not fear-based. Let your soul speak to you of simple love.

ETHICS AND VALUES: CAN THEY BE COMPROMISED?

Some things you won't surrender. No amount of money, power, or fame will move you to compromise your ethics and values.

CHAPTER 4: PURPOSE

❝

*Love
allows you to draw on energy
from "All Creation"
and the entire Universe
becomes your body.*

Too often in society, ethics are moulded, manipulated, and reshaped, depending on the outcome or return sought.

In life you will be tested. Temptations will come along. These temptations are the greatest treason. They test your intellect, will and imagination and have an amazing seductive capacity. Don't redefine everything in your eyes to make it right. Hold your values and seek and speak truth above all.

The greatest thing we must seek in this century, despite having access to almost anything we want, is spirituality, a yearning for something deeper. What we seek and need is intimacy with the living God, which is love's presence.

Pause for a moment and consider the following statements:

- We are all created equal, endowed by our Creator with qualities of life, liberty and happiness.

- The more you have, the more self-reliant you will be. However, be careful of consumerism. Pursuing this alone will leave you with an empty heart.

- Most problems today originate from deep within us. Dis-ease associated with *mindset*, such as depression and stress-related disorders, are a major health crisis.

- It is only when you realise your own spiritual poverty that you seek salvation. We all need divine intervention.

THINK HELPING—LESS SELLING

In your personal and professional life, think more about helping and less about selling. "He who wins souls is wise."—Proverbs 11:30 (NKJV). This statement speaks of trust and friendship that come through genuine relationship building—not through gimmicks, intimidation, or bluff, but from genuine honesty and integrity.

CHAPTER 4: PURPOSE

❝

*There comes a time
when you stop trying to fit in,
seeking approval,
desperately wanting to be liked,
or even hoping that you are understood.
You simply say
"I'm not competing with you anymore...."
You delight and flourish is not fitting in
and prefer to keep the mystery about you
rather than being understood.
Then you really feel alive.*

Contrary to what we are being told by popular culture about marketing yourself and selling your business services, it is actually simpler than we anticipate or expect it to be. When you succeed in building genuine relationships (business or personal), you won't need to sell yourself. People will be drawn to you personally and professionally and what you have to offer.

The way to build genuine relationships is by being the authentic you. It means making a stand for what you believe in and then living your life in alignment with it. When you do this from a heartfelt space of genuine care and belief, you will build loyal and genuine relationships that will propel you further than you can expect.

The secret to your success and growth is to help others succeed and grow. Success isn't just about what you accomplish in your life. It's about how you help others accomplish what they want in their lives.

TO BE TRULY FULFILLED, WE NEED OTHERS

In today's performance-driven culture, we are encouraged to be independent, competitive and highly successful. We compare ourselves to others, examining their success, their wealth, their friends, their jobs, or their bodies. This mindset is based on a false premise: that there is a finite pie of success to be had.

Too often we think about how someone can help us rather than how we can help them. There is wonderful freedom and grace in knowing there is not a finite pie of success. Encourage and support others. Their success will be a blessing to you and vice versa. The relationships in our lives are like an ecosystem that can be sustained only with sufficient nurturing.

Sure, it is important to build the idea of individual responsibility, commitment and achievement, but at the same time we should continue to value and cultivate healthy interdependence.

CHAPTER 4: PURPOSE

*Everyone
wants the truth
but no one
wants to be honest.*

Our greatest joys in life are not often found in living a solitary life. Inherently, we know we have been designed to live for something greater than ourselves.

Interdependence is God's design. Compassion is the awareness of interdependence, which:

- Prevents arrogance;

- Develops accountability;

- Helps us learn and mature;

- Gives us purpose.

CHAPTER 5

. . .

A PERSONAL EXPERIENCE

Vulnerability is my birthplace of joy, creativity, belonging, love and self-acceptance.

Over the past few years I have been on a personal quest to get to know myself intimately. What I realised in the process is sometimes we go through life thinking we know ourselves, but what we know is the persona of who we think we should be.

Sometimes due to circumstances out of our control or decisions we have made, we end up living a life less fulfilling than what we intended. As a result, we can lose our joy, happiness and gratitude. We become busy avoiding our true selves because we believe realness requires weakness of character.

This is how to perceive vulnerability. Do not be afraid to tell your story with all your heart. In doing so, vulnerability gives you freedom to be who you are.

When you are totally open, with nothing to hide, all your energy flows effortlessly into the amazing person you are meant to be.

Consider these wonderful lessons learnt:

Vulnerability:

- Shows courage and strength to pursue dreams;

- Creates authentic, deep bonds and relationships;

- Enables you to grow emotionally and spiritually;

- Gives you back your freedom.

So, if you are faced with a moment of vulnerability, don't allow yourself to retreat to your safe haven. Instead, embrace it wholeheartedly and in doing so, get to know intimately the wonderful, amazing person you are.

CHAPTER 5: A PERSONAL EXPETIENCE

"

*A child's self-esteem and happiness
are not based on what you give them,
nor is it based on the quality time
that you spend with them.
It is based on how you RECEIVE
their contribution,
their stories and their love.*

CHAPTER 5: A PERSONAL EXPETIENCE

A CHILD'S PERSPECTIVE: UNINHIBITED, RAW AND TRUE

I wish to share with you a personal moment with my daughter, aged seven. She said to me one morning as we were getting ready for school, "Mummy, I am going to save all my money so when I grow up I can visit all the poor countries in the world and give them my money to help the people that don't have many things".

"That's beautiful," I said to her, "but honey, that will take a lot of time to visit each country and some are far away. You can just make what's called a *donation* to charity and the money will go to them to help them."

She replied, "Mummy, it's not just about giving the money. You have to see them and talk to them, play with them, and make them laugh. Then you are helping them for real life."

"Wow!" I say. So much insight from a seven year old. How often have you given a donation and felt good, thinking you have done your good deed for the day or year? Don't get me wrong, donations are absolutely essential. I encourage you to continue to donate to your charity, and if you have never done so, make a donation today because together we can make an impression.

But don't feel that by having done that it's now not your problem and you have done all you can. Too many people in this world think that by making a donation they are off the hook. They have contributed to society. It makes them feel good, yet somehow, they don't give the situation another thought.

Sometimes we think that by making a financial donation, we don't have to do anything more. It takes our accountability away.

Get involved. See what you can do in your own community to make a difference. Volunteer, spend some time with someone less fortunate, share a cup of tea with someone who feels isolated such as an elderly neighbour. Help someone with their shopping, cleaning or running errands.

CHAPTER 5: A PERSONAL EXPETIENCE

"

A mother's love is boundless.
She awakens a deep yearning
to love and be loved.
Her capacity for healing,
building resilience and awakening
hope, imagination and courage
cannot and should not be underestimated.
And although at times her heart breaks, the
more she gives of her infinite love,
the more she feels this infinite love.

Financial support via donations is absolutely essential, and I sincerely thank you for your continued contribution. But it does not take away our accountability. Nor does it always fix everything. It does not mend the broken heart of a hurting soul. As a human race, what we most seek is genuine intimate contact with someone that shows us they truly care. The problems of the world cannot be changed unless we awaken the beautiful hearts in the world.

Compassion, love, grace and humility are God's beautiful language. It is so refreshing when a seven year old can put the things that matter most in life in perspective and remind her grown-up mum. Thank you, gorgeous girl. You are a blessing.

A CHILD'S INSIGHT: HOW BLESSED

I would also like to share with you a very personal moment with my seven-year-old daughter at bedtime one night.

"Mummy you are the best!"
"Thank you honey, why do you say that?"
"Because, Mummy:
You are a doctor. You help me when I'm sick.
You are a cook. You make me nice food.
You are a teacher. You help me with my homework.
You are a dentist. You took my tooth out.
You are a cleaner. You clean the house.
You are a taxi. You drive me everywhere.
You are a helper. You help grandma when she's sick.
You are a dancer. You dance ballet with me.

CHAPTER 5: A PERSONAL EXPETIENCE

You are enough!

You are a singer. You sing with me.
You are funny. You make me laugh.
You make me happy, Mummy."

We often miss what we already are and chase what we think we need to be. Look within to find the beautiful person you already are and show gratitude for the wonderful things you can do. Life sometimes gets complicated as we get older. Bring it back to simplicity and observe your life through the innocence of a child— your inner child. Life is a blessing.

ENDURING LOVE

I feel truly blessed to have witnessed the showing of the most amazing gesture of love, compassion, patience, and care. As I waited in a doctor's surgery with my daughter some time ago, I observed an elderly couple. They both looked in their late seventies. As it turned out, he was 89 and his gorgeous wife was 85.

What impressed me the most and has left a profound mark in my heart, was the amazing love this gentleman had for his wife. It was not the words he spoke, but what went unspoken: the way he held her hand, the way he looked into her eyes as if he was looking deep within her soul, the way he helped her put her jacket on. It was the comforting arm he had on her shoulder to support her and reassure her that everything was going to be okay.

His wife was showing early signs of Alzheimer's disease. She was enamored by my little girl and they had a wonderful chat and enjoyed each other's company.

I spoke to the gentleman for some time. His story was an amazing journey of strength, inspiration, and courage. I asked him what his secret was. "We have been married 66 years, and each year I have loved her more than the last."

CHAPTER 5: A PERSONAL EXPETIENCE

"

The best thing you can do for your children
is increase your own happiness.
Conditioned to think
that parenting is mostly about providing "things",
doing "things" and the like,
we forget about our own needs
to the point of exhaustion
and frustration with our own life.
Children model their behaviour
on what they see.
The most loving thing you can do
for your children
is to love and care for yourself.
If you don't look after your happiness,
your children will take that burden on
and try to do it for you
as if somehow,
they are responsible for your life.

Wow! Enduring love. How wonderful and amazing to know it still exists. An unconditional love based on trust, respect, and freedom.

> *"Love bears all things, believes all things, hopes all things, endures all things."*
>
> —1Corinthians 13:7 (ESV)

CHAPTER 6

·

·

·

HEALTH AND WELLNESS

YOUR JOURNEY TO HEALTH AND WELLNESS STARTS NOW

I truly understand sometimes the thought of embarking on a health and fitness journey can be daunting, confusing and frankly too hard!

An overwhelming amount of often contradictory information exists regarding how to exercise, what to eat, what to do and what not to do. The thought of squeezing into Lycra tights and signing up to a gym can be overwhelming and confronting. The end result maybe that you quit before you've started.

Health and wellness are not a one-size-fits-all matter. It may be for you a matter of weight loss, fitness, strength, stress relief, social interaction, or more specific activities to help achieve specific outcomes. There is no right or wrong answer and the key here is to find out what it means for *you* and to take ownership and responsibility for it.

What I am referring to is simply taking that initial step to get the body moving. Listen to your body and find what works for you and your situation. Get active, go for a walk, swim, bike ride, or join a dance studio. Find something you like. Then you are more likely to keep up with it. Of course, to make a change to your body and achieve long-lasting results, it takes sheer hard work, consistency and commitment to your goals.

Your exercise and nutrition will evolve over time. I think it is important when you first embark on this journey to work on introducing small changes at a time, to work consistently at that and have fun. Establish a pattern because that's when it merges into a lifestyle choice.

Health and wellness. Take it back to basics:

- Simple, clean eating;

- Get the body moving regularly;

CHAPTER 6: HEALTH AND WELLNESS

❝

*Life is simple... it really is!
Have courage to love
and grace to accept love.*

◎ Have fun;

◎ Nurture, accept and love yourself for who you are.

LISTEN TO YOUR BODY: SOMETIMES YOU JUST HAVE TO *BE*

How often do you push yourself to the point of total physical and mental exhaustion? Do you grab another coffee, eat a doughnut or chocolate bar for energy, consume too much alcohol to lift your mood, or take medication for your tension headache?

We are programmed to be interminably busy, carried away with our everyday responsibilities created by society but mostly by ourselves. We are occupied with work, family, eating well, exercise, staying on top of our game, learning, growing, self-development, empowerment, being successful, accumulating and having a social life. The list goes on. All these are absolutely essential to flourish and contribute to society.

The problem is when we engage in these things to the point of exhaustion and depletion, it often leads to physical and emotional illness. Sometimes we are reluctant to believe that we are taking on more than we are currently capable of, and herein lies the problem.

Your body is amazing. It will respond to everything going on in your life. If you are run down or depleted, you will feel clouded, confused and physically and emotionally unwell and this will compromise your happiness.

It is important to listen to your body. How you take care of yourself fuels your body's innate wisdom to be able to heal and balance itself. Your body is constantly talking to you. You just have to stop and listen.

To heal and stay in balance, remember to nurture and support your body. Be patient, forgiving and be kind to yourself. Know

CHAPTER 6: HEALTH AND WELLNESS

❝

*Self-awareness itself
is the healing.
You are the changemaker
for your own life.*

when you are pushing or demanding too much of yourself and accept that sometimes you just have to *be*.

HAVE YOU FORGOTTEN *WHY* YOU SHOULD BE HAPPY?

It happens to all of us at some stage of our life and sometimes we seem to be on an ongoing quest to find happiness. We may appear to have a great life, great job, nice house and a beautiful family, yet we are unfulfilled. Or we think that once we attain all these things, then we will find happiness.

We hide or mask our unhappiness on the inside with pretend happiness on the outside. We are social butterflies, outspoken and confident, yet we feel disconnected from within. If this is you, I ask you to find a quiet place and just be in stillness. Place your hand on your heart and feel that connection to your soul.

That connection you feel is life and where happiness lives. True happiness is a state of the heart. It's the place where all our dreams, visions, values and beliefs exist. Often when we struggle to be happy, it's because our actions and the way we live on the outside do not align with our inner selves and what we really stand for. This is because society predetermines what we should think, look like, eat, and dress, so we lose courage and faith in our own abilities.

Take a moment to visualize what happiness means to you:

- What does it look like?

- What does it feel like?

- What does it smell like?

- What does it taste like?

- What do you hear when you feel happy?

"

*Self-acceptance changes everything,
it really does!
Not as a one-time experience on a good day,
but an ongoing and deepening practice,
even on your worst day.
Self-acceptance is the ultimate catalyst
for change and growth.
A powerful intelligence,
a profound awakening
which supports you
to embrace all parts of YOU,
encouraging you to embody love
in absolutely every part of your life,
whether it's a good day or not.*

Stillness of your mind brings you back to your soul connection. To find real happiness, reignite your passions, dreams and values and become the person you are meant to be.

WHY HAVE WE OVERCOMPLICATED HEALTHY LIVING?

Information overload! There's a new diet, exercise program and pill sold each week as a quick fix. We often hear the saying: "Healthy living is a lifestyle change and not a destination." Yet we continue to research and seek a short-term fix.

The *key* to wellness is to accept *personal responsibility* for your health and well-being. No diet pill, workout program, personal trainer, protein shake, gym membership, or diet plan can give you that! Stop comparing yourself to others and focus on what works for *you*.

Let's take it back to basics. Healthy living should be about:

- Personal accountability;
- Balance;
- Simple clean eating;
- Getting the body moving regularly;
- Emotional well-being and mindset;
- Nurturing, accepting and loving yourself for who you are.

"

*Living in the past
nurtures regret
and living in the future
nurtures fear.
Authenticity and awareness
are your true friends
and awaken your consciousness
to live in the NOW!*

WALK AND TALK CLUB: START NOW

Lift your mood and feel great!

Accountability + Routine = Positive results for health

Connect with amazing women and men whilst you talk health tips and life matters.

BFF (Best Friends in Fitness) bringing a community of men and women together in fitness and life! Inspire your BFF's to get moving!

Benefits of regular walking:

- Weight loss;
- Increased metabolism;
- Healthier heart;
- Increased self-esteem;
- Toned muscles;
- Increased energy;
- Stronger bones and joints;
- Relief from stress;
- Reduced risk of high blood pressure;
- Improved mindset;
- Positive outlook.

> *The ultimate universal language*
> *that connects all souls*
> *is the spoken and unspoken language of love.*
> *Truth is love's translator*
> *that opens the way for you*
> *to speak such language*
> *with ease and flow.*

SEEKING A MAKEOVER TO MAKE YOU FEEL BETTER?

As women, usually when we think of a makeover, we think spa treatment, makeup, hair style, manicure, new clothes, or jewellery. We often look for ways to transform ourselves on the outside. So much of our effort is focused on our outward appearance to make us feel better.

However, outer beauty becomes meaningless if our inner beauty is flawed. When we are lacking from within, outer focus only masks our pain.

To experience the ultimate makeover like never before, pay attention to the tips below. You'll experience a glow that no outer makeover can give you and will make others notice and say, "I want what she's having".

- *Open your heart to love:* A love based on compassion, respect for your life and acceptance of your past.

- *Reach out and influence:* Speak words that edify others, not tear them down.

- *Renew your thoughts:* Your thoughts predetermine the quality of your life.

- *Awaken your soul:* Have courage and faith to follow your dreams and stand in your truth.

Experience an ultimate makeover that will open your heart to a new truth, a new joy, a new love and a new way of life.

HEALTH AND WELLNESS IS MORE THAN A WEIGHT LOSS JOURNEY

Health and wellness, in particular weight loss, are related to our identity. Weight problems are usually evidence of a conflict over who we are and the actions we take. When these two are mis-

*Let your emotions
be like the misty rains falling
that fill the lake with serenity.
Emotions are a meandering river
that connect and fill
the hearts of humanity
with a gentle energy of peace.*

aligned, we face internal conflict, which leads to stress and emotional eating, which leads in turn to an unhealthy relationship with food, lack of motivation to maintain a healthy lifestyle and feeling stuck.

It's no secret that the key to long-term health and wellness is changing our emotional perspective. To do this we must look at our internal environment and structure and people around us being our circle of influence. This includes our core foundations, beliefs and highest values.

Change the lens of how you view yourself, your circumstances, your environment, your relationships with others and the world as a whole. Health and wellness can be a wonderful journey, not only to lose some unwanted kilos but also to find yourself.

WHY YOU SHOULD NOT SKIP BREAKFAST

Some people skip breakfast in an effort to lose weight. But that's not a good idea. *Why?*

Skipping meals, especially breakfast, can make you gain weight! Skipping breakfast often makes you consume larger portions at the next meal or nibble throughout the day on high-calorie snacks that are high in fat and sugar but that have little or no nutritional value.

Skipping breakfast can make you feel more tired, irritable, and restless in the morning and sometimes throughout the day. People who eat breakfast have better concentration and energy and are more efficient throughout the day.

People often tell me that they get hungrier throughout the day if they eat breakfast. I say that's a great thing because it kick-starts the metabolism and boosts your energy and mood, so you feel inspired to get your body moving and make better choices.

CHAPTER 6: HEALTH AND WELLNESS

"

Love sustains Life...
Where there is Love, there is Life,
Where there is Life, there is Love.

Wake up your metabolism and start your day with a healthy breakfast! When combined with healthy meals and snacks throughout the day, together with regular exercise and movement, it keeps it firing all day, making it perfect for weight loss and maintenance.

NAKED PERSPECTIVE: HOW DO YOU REALLY SEE YOURSELF?

Pause for a minute and think honestly about your thoughts today. Are you tearing down yourself-worth, feeling ashamed of your past or present circumstances?

Are you defining your value based on your body shape and appearance?

Are you setting unrealistic standards for yourself, seeking unattainable perfection and then feeling like you failed?

Are you seeking the approval of others, chasing love?

Are you giving away your power and waiting for others to elevate you and determine your value?

Are you sacrificing your own identity to fit in and gain acceptance?

Are you controlled by an unhealthy relationship with food? Do you overeat or starve yourself?

Are you feeling responsible for others in your life and taking on their loads, friends, children, partners, or co-workers to the point where you don't let your own light shine?

Your spiritual inheritance is one of *forgiveness*. It is this truth that gives you unconditional love and hope. Free yourself from these self-destructive thought patterns. It is through God's grace that He heals us and this brings freedom to live a new life.

"

*Smile,
if for no other reason than just because...
because your heart sings a beautiful song
and because your soul knows
the meaning of that song;
LOVE.*

IMAGINE THE POSSIBILITIES

Imagine your life with an abundance of creativity, allowing your being and your self-expression to radiate from deep within you and outwards to positively affect you and others in your life. Imagine being able to accept your inner truth, your deepest and most honest desires, and allowing these ideas to blossom into unrestricted greatness in the world. This is possible for you are unique and have a special gift to offer the world.

Every moment in your life up to this stage was meant to happen exactly the way it has happened. Who you are now is as a result of all these events and experiences transpiring and true change begins when you can accept these moments in truth and respect?

Only then will your path illuminate forward towards happiness and greatness.

Life is a journey. It has a beginning and an end and everything in between is *your* story. Don't devalue it for it is valuable and has the capacity to make a difference in the world. We all have a responsibility to live a life that is of help and inspiration to others.

What do you want to be remembered for?

CHAPTER 7

.

.

.

HOW TO MAKE A CHANGE

OPENING THE DOOR TO CHANGE

Your mindset has the ability to distort your perception of reality and ultimately sabotage your potential. It is the key to opening the door to change and unlocking your potential to be at your personal best.

To help maintain mental well-being, consider these tips:

- Eat balanced, healthy food;
- Get the body moving regularly;
- Sleep well;
- Plan and prioritise your day;
- Switch off your electronic devices;
- Connect with others in the community and belong;
- Cultivate a healthy environment, including friends and family;
- Consume alcohol moderately;
- Stimulate your mind with hobbies, reading and the like;
- Ensure *you time!*

STEP OUT OF CHAOS AND INTO HARMONY

A disconnect in your relationship with yourself can cause chaos and disorder in your life, resulting in a deterioration of your health and well-being. This may provoke physical health issues resulting from your inability to maintain a healthy lifestyle. Emotional chaos may also result in dis-ease and in some cases mental illness such as stress and anxiety and in more severe cases depression, which is not often spoken about.

CHAPTER 7: HOW TO MAKE A CHANGE

"

*Your words will make people feel and question,
in a world that tells them not to.
You are tasked with speaking gentle words,
powerful words, courageous words,
playful words, creative words,
compassionate words, words of strength,
words of truth, words of freedom,
words of love—unity of all.
The magnitude of such beauty
creates movement and motion
that will help people rediscover
their heart one more time.
This is your greatest responsibility of all.*

When we are disconnected, we feel unloved, unsupported and alone. We adopt a fight or flight pattern, which is a survival state and continue to live life in that way. This places immense stress on us physically and emotionally and often our pattern is to escape this pain through more painful methods.

The human experience is a journey to find love, security and harmony. By enriching your connection to your heart, you will improve your well-being and bring harmony to your life.

Don't be afraid to speak your truth and become the person you were always meant to be. Don't be afraid to pursue your dreams and do so with a renewed strength and passion. Sure, it may upset some people in your life; in fact, I guarantee it will. This process and journey will reveal true and loyal friendships.

The universal energy of love is the one energy that will awaken you and free you to be who you really are and this brings peace and harmony.

GET OUT OF THE TOXIC RELATIONSHIP WITH YOURSELF

Dig deep and be honest with yourself. What is your current emotional state of mind?

Do you find it difficult to control your emotions and as a result engage in toxic behaviour or have an unhealthy relationship with food? We all go through things in life. This is not to shame or judge you.

Whatever your situation, know that it is absolutely possible to move past that point and live a life of amazing inner peace, love and gratitude.

Toxic behaviours are often a direct result of an unhealthy emotional state of being, which is usually evidence of the conflict be-

CHAPTER 7: HOW TO MAKE A CHANGE

> *Wisdom does not come from age,*
> *knowledge, or as some people think*
> *status, position nor title.*
> *Wisdom comes from doing things;*
> *failing, getting back up*
> *and doing more things*
> *but under no circumstances giving up.*
> *No philosophy, mantra or advice*
> *will hold true for every conceivable situation.*
> *You have to experience it*
> *to learn the lesson.*

tween who we are and the actions we take. When these are misaligned, we face internal conflict that leads to stress, and if we are not equipped to deal with this stress, it leads to toxic, unhealthy behaviour.

Next time you feel a deep, obsessive, uncontrollable anxiety and seek instant gratification to sooth the pain in your soul, take a step back and consider why you are doing what you are doing. What lies beneath your pain?

To manage your emotions, often it takes rebuilding the core foundations of your being rather than just mending the cracks and repainting the wall. This process involves rediscovering what are your highest values and beliefs and making sure you live your life in accordance with what they are.

Here are some tips to get started in this process:

- Do some honest self-reflection;

- Do not blame or judge yourself;

- Identify the issues affecting your life;

- Work on small changes; keep it simple;

- Don't compare;

- Release your fears;

- Focus on what is important to *you;*

- Seek professional help if necessary.

You are a brilliant and unique creation and are destined for greatness. Make a decision that goes through every fibre of your muscle that you will make a change *today* and that no matter what, you will never, ever, *ever* give up.

CHAPTER 7: HOW TO MAKE A CHANGE

"

*In many ways
we are seeing the veil of fear is lifting.
Something very real is opening up
what seems to be impossible.
Remove the veil so that you might see
what is really happening around you
and not be intoxicated by stories,
drama and fear.
You're in this moment for a reason.
Continue to point the way
to those luminous truths.*

CHAPTER 7: HOW TO MAKE A CHANGE

TO BE REMEMBERED

Rather than just aiming to get through the day, week, month, or year, flourish in the moment and run with endurance the race that is set before you.

If coping in a toxic world seems to be on your mind most of the time, you may have forgotten about yourself. *Self-care* is the new buzzword, but what does it mean? Self-care is about looking after yourself daily, including your emotional well-being, by managing stress and maintaining a healthy lifestyle. When you look after yourself physically and emotionally, you are in a better place to cope with what life throws at you.

Consider these tips for your self-care:

- Get your body moving on a regular basis;
- Eat simply and cleanly using fresh ingredients;
- Factor in regular "me time;" do what you love doing;
- Be kind to yourself;
- Accept your imperfections;
- Let go of what you can't control;
- Open your heart to love;
- Walk away from toxic situations and friendships;
- Stand in your truth;
- Find your voice; don't be afraid to have an opinion;
- Laugh and smile a lot;
- Never, ever give up on your dreams.

You are *royalty* and you deserve the *best*.

CHAPTER 7: HOW TO MAKE A CHANGE

"

*Throughout our lives,
we are constantly being sculpted
into who we are
by those we choose to surround ourselves with.
Consider for a moment,
who is in your circle of influence?*

GET BACK ON TRACK

Were you committed—excited—when you set your New Year's resolutions this year? Has that resolve fizzled out now?

It's time to take another look at the goals you set this year. What were they? Did they include improved health and wellness, weight loss, better relationships, self-care, career change, setting healthy boundaries, fitness, or personal development? If your goals no longer resonate with you, I suggest you connect within yourself and rediscover your heart's desire.

When we fail to stay on track with our goals, it's often because we are disconnected from what they actually mean to us. On the other hand, if you are still passionate about your goals but have fallen off the wagon, it is not too late. Pick yourself up, dust your knees and get back on with determination. Connect your goals with what you want your life to look like.

Consider your setback just that: a *temporary* setback. Never, ever, *ever* give up on your goals. Quitting is not an option.

Consider these tips to help you get back on track for your goals this year:

- Evaluate yourself to discover where you are now.

- Awaken your inspiration and reaffirm it each day.

- Set realistic goals.

- Remove fear. Stop comparing yourself to others.

- Don't seek perfection. It's about achieving your personal best.

> *It takes someone who understands*
> *the tone of your heart beat*
> *to be able to dance*
> *to the music of your love.*

LIFE IS A BLANK CANVAS: WHAT WILL YOU PAINT?

Paint something beautiful and of worth that is aligned with your highest values and with living your dream.

Are you painting on an old, worn-out canvas that has lost its vibrancy, strength and colour? If you don't like what you see, the picture looks tired. Start a blank canvas. Yes, it's okay to do that. You're not quitting, you're just changing the artwork.

Make a decision today to get a blank canvas and start to paint something different. Start with an area of your life that you want to make a change to—maybe your health, fitness, finances, relationships, or career—and decide how you'd like it to look. Choose the right thoughts because they will become your habits. Your habits will transform your vision and create the masterpiece of your life.

A true masterpiece is created from the heart. If your artwork is not a reflection of your deepest heart's desires, I encourage you to let go of the old, tired-looking canvas. Let go of what you know and step out of your comfort zone. Make sure what you are creating is *your* masterpiece and not someone else's idea of what your life should look like.

Transcend what people tell you is impossible. Deep within your heart there is something magical waiting to be expressed. You are the artist, and your heart is your paintbrush. Go ahead and design your masterpiece. The entire universe is your blank canvas, and your life is your artwork.

TO LIVE GRATEFULLY: A MALE PERSPECTIVE

To all you gorgeous women who have connected with my posts and messages, I ask you to give a copy of this book to a male figure in your life: a father, a partner, a friend, or a brother who you feel may benefit from its messages.

CHAPTER 7: HOW TO MAKE A CHANGE

"

*If you could only feel
the tenderness of Complete Love,
you would know you are safe
and loved beyond measure.
Surrender to your journey.*

Even though we have come a long way from our parents' childhood days, in most places society's view of a male's role is still to be a hunter and gatherer, or a breadwinner. Society judges a man based on his bank account, car, house, success, leadership and by the woman on his arm. There is pressure on males to be in control, tough, dominant and self-reliant and they are expected to succeed both professionally and socially.

Such expectations exert pressures on men that often result in a huge disconnect. Disconnection from your true self makes it challenging to show *love* and *respect* to those around you, including family, friends and loved ones.

If you are one of these men who is facing difficult circumstances, ask yourself: *What do I most desire? What are my highest values? Am I living a life congruent with my highest values? Can I express my vulnerability easily? Is my life an expression of love?* Pursue these honest answers, irrespective of society's expectations and live by these rules for your emotional and spiritual well-being:

- *Live outwardly.* It's okay to be vulnerable and show emotion.

- *Live generously.* It's okay to share your thoughts and feelings.

- *Live authentically.* It's okay to be the real you.

- *Live faithfully.* It's okay to have faith in life's journey.

TURN DOWN THE NOISE IN YOUR LIFE—TO REVEAL YOUR TRUTH

Noise in the form of distractions from social media, electronic gadgets and expectations from friends and family, which all cause clutter in your mind, can affect your health and well-being. It's easy to lose perspective if you immerse yourself in the noise around you. This can make you feel tense, worried, angry, afraid, and frustrated and leave you flying on autopilot.

CHAPTER 7: HOW TO MAKE A CHANGE

❝

Life is simple...
it really is...
Have courage to love
and grace to accept love.

Noise is a distraction to your highest self. If you have chosen to live in a noisy world in order to avoid the confrontation of your truth, ask yourself honestly:

- Am I holding friendships together that fell apart a long time ago?

- Am I apologizing for who I am and the choices I have made?

- Am I seeking the support and validation of others in order to pursue my dreams?

- Am I hiding your authentic self for fear of being judged?

- Am I people-pleasing, including my family and friends, in order to avoid a confrontation?

If you are living within the safe parameters of your comfort zone in order to avoid disappointing family, friends and loved ones, I urge you to find courage. Also:

- Speak your truth—even if it displeases those closest to you. Truth is about expressing what you think and feel in an authentic, vulnerable, transparent way.

- Stop managing their emotions. You cannot prevent other people from experiencing pain, disappointment, or discomfort. That's their issue to deal with.

- Make a conscious decision to reduce the noise level in your life. Creativity and self-expression require stillness of your mind.

- Ask in stillness; listen in stillness to reveal your truth. With this comes your freedom and inner peace.

CHAPTER 7: HOW TO MAKE A CHANGE

❝

*Be loving and respectful
to all individuals
and you will attract individuals
that will love and respect you back.*

YOUR THOUGHTS PREDETERMINE THE QUALITY OF YOUR LIFE

Your thoughts are what make you the person that you are, not your ethnicity, occupation, wealth, or status. Your thoughts are central to your life; they are what define you as a person.

Thoughts tend to become negative and can create walls. The greatest prison cells in all the world are made with the most convincing thoughts. These are diseases of the mind: fear, anxiety, melancholy, shame, judgement and feeling not good enough. When things happen to us, we think it's the beginning of the end of the world.

If you change your action alone, you can do so for a day or so. Thoughts precede actions and therefore become more important than the actions themselves. Renew your mindset to make lasting change. You can change your life by changing the way you think. Where your thoughts are today is where your life will be tomorrow.

Our minds were created to be full of life, potential, brilliance, hope, generosity, planning and dreaming. You are a brilliant and unique creation. Surrender your fears and negative thoughts to experience a renewed lease on life, passion and determination. Live the kind of life intended for you, an oasis of peace and tranquillity.

TRANSFORMATION STARTS IN THE MIND

Just as our senses present a landscape for our body to touch, feel, smell, see and taste, our thoughts present a view of life that influence soul decisions about what we will do and who we will be.

When we change our beliefs, we transform our thoughts about what is possible. Freedom lies in knowing that ultimately the power lies within each of us to make a change. You can make a difference today. Your time as a caterpillar has expired. Your wings are ready. Now fly.

*Simple acts
with the purest intentions
bring profound joy and happiness.
Engage your will
and move away from any expectation.
This state of being
frees you to experience gratitude
for the simple things.*

UNCLUTTER YOUR MIND: UNCLUTTER YOUR LIFE

Clutter is found not just in your home, office, car and wardrobe. Clutter also exists in your mind. It has the potential to distract you from living a meaningful life filled with purpose, passion and determination.

Self-reflection is the first step to uncluttering your mind, and this requires *stillness* of your mind and body.

Find a quiet spot, focus on your breathing, and observe how you feel as you reflect:

- Accept where you are now;
- Be kind to yourself;
- Work on small changes;
- Keep it simple;
- Don't compare. Release your fears;
- Visualize what's important to you. *Own* it!
- *Let go* of everything else.

YOUR SMILE IS MORE PRECIOUS THAN ANY DIAMOND

Your smile has the power to influence someone's perspective and provide hope. It can change their world and as a result change your world, too.

Isn't that the greatest gift of all?

CHAPTER 7: HOW TO MAKE A CHANGE

"

*Listen in stillness
and in that quietude
find acceptance for your past,
gratitude for your present
and renewed hope for your future.*

Your smile is universal. It speaks all languages.
Your smile is the language of kindness.
Your smile transcends all barriers,
including age, race, and culture.
Your smile is infectious. Spread it around.
Your smile speaks more than your words ever will.
Your smile is the most luminous makeup you can wear.
Your smile costs you nothing.
Your smile radiates a glow brighter than the sun.
Your smile is the one key that fits the lock of all hearts.
Your smile is like a boomerang.
It will always come back to you.

DISCOVER WHO ARE YOU

You are a multi-dimensional being. Many layers make up who you are. It goes way deeper than your physical appearance and the way you act with your conscious mind. Consider the analogy of an iceberg: What you see on top is not all there is to the iceberg. Under the surface there is way more mass than the eye will ever see. This mirrors your unconscious mind.

Your unconscious mind is the largest and most powerful part of who you are. It holds all your memories, beliefs and thoughts, and is where you connect with spirit and your authentic self. Your life is much more than what society and culture paint it to be.

Turn down the noise that creates clutter and distraction in your life and step into that great being inside of you that is boundless

*The highest choice
is not always the choice
which seems to serve another.
In fact, quite possibly
your choice will disappoint the other.
This does not mean you are selfish,
it means you are self aware.*

and knows freedom. Choose to live without fear and regret. Liberate yourself from the confines of your past and limited thinking. Return to the source and re-establish your connection. Experience the magic of staying in your energy and being in your truth.

LISTEN TO YOUR SOUL

Why should we do that? Because we get attached to places, material things and people who we think we should be or who we are expected to be! Fear takes over and we prefer to stay within the safe parameters of our comfort zone, even though they may not necessarily be safe parameters.

Consider the times you ignored your soul's guidance. Chances are you did because you thought you should in order to please others. Society is quick to judge about what we should and shouldn't do, so we talk ourselves out of making changes.

When we don't listen to our inner selves, our lives end up in chaos and disorder. We experience painful interventions and emotional strain, including stress, anxiety and even loss and illness.

Listening to yourself is necessary to shift towards action and self-realization. In the process you face the truth about who you are and what is in line for your true higher self. Today, take a step back from your thoughts and become the observer. Tap into your intuitive senses and let your inner guidance speak. You'll know the truth by the way you feel.

ACCEPT YOUR LIFE UNCONDITIONALLY

The most amazing things happen when you accept yourself unconditionally. Love and respect yourself for who you are, and live by your values, not someone elses.

CHAPTER 7: HOW TO MAKE A CHANGE

"

*Give yourself permission to feel,
to want something more,
to expect something more,
to believe that you deserve
something more in life.*

PRACTICAL STEPS TO MAKE A CHANGE

In order to have a renewed lease on life, passion and determination:

- Self-evaluate where you are now.
- Know that you have everything you need within you to succeed.
- Happiness is a state of mind — a choice to make.
- Awaken your inspiration and reaffirm it each day.
- Set realistic goals.
- Remove fear. Stop comparing yourself to others.
- Ask for professional help as needed.
- Make small changes at a time.
- Monitor and track your progress.
- Buddy up. Instigate a circle of influence.
- Most importantly, never, ever, *ever* give up!

NEVER, EVER, EVER GIVE UP

The strongest factor for long term success is *self-belief*:

- Believing you can do it;
- Believing you deserve it;
- Never, ever, *ever* giving up!

CHAPTER 7: HOW TO MAKE A CHANGE

"

*Consider that
your own resolve,
courage and purposefulness
to always do your best,
to never give up
and to not merely accept the status quo
is way, way more important
than the outcome of these things.*

CHAPTER 7: HOW TO MAKE A CHANGE

My mantra is this:

> What matters is not the person I am when times are easy, but the person I become when times are tough. That sort of person is what defines us and makes us stronger and more determined to succeed. We have a tough journey. It was not meant to be easy.
>
> Consider doing a spring cleaning. Filter your friendships, so all you are left with is loyal, trustworthy friends that you can always depend on. Clarify your goals and direction and set yourself on a path of awesome success. You will get through it. *Believe!*

THANK YOU

.

.

.

THANK YOU

To my dearest Tim

We are the authors of our unforgettable love story. I'm so excited to be journeying through life with you and can't wait to write our next chapter together.

Love always Xx

THANK YOU

"

*Gratitude
is like sunshine for the soul.
It helps you blossom
where you're planted.*

—*Mirjana*

THANK YOU

I have deep gratitude for God, for the salvation, restoration and renewal of my life. I am so blessed to be on this journey with the faith I hold so dear. This book is testimony to His wonderful work in my life. God has a plan for your life, too.

I thank my amazing children Danny, Caroline, Tiana and Emily for their unconditional love and support. These angels are a gift from God and I am grateful for the honour of being their mummy and seeing them blossom in their own most incredible ways.

To my gorgeous daughter-in law Manuela, thank you for your love, support and inspiration. To my dearest friend, co-creator and confidant Shannon Dunn, thank you for your love and all that we've shared, forever grateful.

Thank you to all people in my life, those who have come and gone and those who have stayed and to those who are on their way and yet to come. I thank you for your love, for the experiences shared and for the valuable lessons learned and gift of insight and knowing.

I wish to honor and thank Sara Salomon for her creative artistry in the book design and cover. Thank you Emma Nally for the beautiful symbols that give depth to the meaning of the words.

ABOUT THE AUTHOR

.

.

.

ABOUT THE AUTHOR

Mirjana Boznovska is a human behaviouralist authority and conscious leadership expert, supporting people of all ages to reach their ultimate potential, personally and professionally. Her innate ability to teach and mentor with deep insight and intuition has earned her the titles of visionary, thought leader, game-changer and future-shaper.

The mother-of-four draws upon her depth of life experience, business successes and high level practitioner training to help empower people to think differently about themselves and others—to be the light.

Mirjana is a Master Neuro Linguistic Programming (NLP) practitioner and trainer, corporate trainer and consultant, as well as emotional intelligence specialist.

These skills enable her to be the catalyst for her clients' expanded awareness and potential.

As an author, writer and heart-led speaker, Mirjana reaches people on a soul level, awakening an understanding of each person's personal power and abilities, so they see their own divinity and wisdom within.

As a conscious-minded social media influencer, Mirjana's work reaches people around the world.

Her popular and highly-engaged Facebook community puts forth high quality content that enables her audience to challenge and change their personal status quos in order to live their best lives. The ripple effect from Mirjana's work is a new wave of conscious-minded change-makers and business leaders who are, in turn, influencing the leaders of tomorrow.

Her one-on-one leadership coaching enables men and women to embrace their authentic power, while her corporate consultancy expertise reaches beyond the current paradigms to create genuine shift in the way businesses operate, in order to foster leadership at every level.

ABOUT THE AUTHOR

ABOUT THE AUTHOR

Mirjana's ethos and calling is centred around every person feeling empowered, without looking to others for validation. She supports her clients and followers to be at their best physically, emotionally and spiritually—sparking a capacity to show up in the world with love, compassion and truth.

"Irrespective of field or career, these highest values set the strongest foundation for a more meaningful, purposeful life," Mirjana says.

Mirjana's bespoke programs reach executives, visionaries, CEOs, teams and beyond, helping foster personal leadership enhancement, business and career mastery, relationship success, genius flow and creativity, as well as physical, spiritual and emotional empowerment for happiness and fulfilment.

"This is an expansive way of approaching work and business life—with limitless potential as it taps into the Universal Mind rather than the social mind. It is the latter we have been conditioned to follow and believe as truth. This fallacy stifles our potential as it is limiting and conditional. It is time for a new way."

The *Live Gratefully* author is currently writing her next book, *Be the Light*.

ABOUT THE AUTHOR

MIRJANA'S SPECIALTIES INCLUDE:

- Master Neuro Linguistic programming;
- Master Neuro Linguistic training;
- Archetypal coaching;
- Transformation and influencer coaching;
- Keynote presentations;
- Conscious leadership modelling;
- Business mastery;
- Entrepreneurial success;
- Conscious-minded team culture;
- Self-empowerment;
- Career mastery;
- Conscious parenting;

ABOUT THE AUTHOR

- Stress management;
- Mind and body wellness;
- Personal and professional development;
- Goal setting;
- The art of self-love;
- Relationship communication and nurturing;
- Authentic success, love and happiness;
- Be-Do-Have paradigm embodiment.

Mirjana Boznovska is available worldwide for:

- Guest speaking.
- Inspirational business coaching.
- Corporate Leadership courses.

ABOUT THE AUTHOR

INQUIRIES:

Join Mirjana and the
Mirjana community at: **❶** */mirjanalight*

For introspection,
videos and insights: **◉** */mirjanalight*

Be inspired and subscribe: **⊕** *www.mirjana.co*

For one-on-one consultations
or group corporate leadership   **✉** *mirjana@mirjana.co*
programs, please email:

Shannon Dunn, Publicist: **✉** *shannon@shannondunn.com*

www.ingramcontent.com/pod-product-compliance
Lightning Source LLC
Chambersburg PA
CBHW041610220426
43667CB00004B/61